Welcome to Our Humble Commode

Light-Hearted Tales of Family, Home, and Growing Faith

Randy Fishell

Copyright © 2009 by Randy Fishell
All rights reserved, including the right to
reproduce this book or portions thereof in any form.

Cover and back cover illustrations copyright © 2009 by Randy Fishell. All Bible quotations are from the *New International Version*.

ISBN 978-0-578-02324-3

Foreword

"Dad, I want to live all of my life."

I've chewed on this remark by our then-five-year-old son. I think what Andrew meant is that he hopes to draw breath well into his retirement years. But pondering his comment pointed me in the direction of an important truth: it is indeed possible to zip through life without *really* living.

For me, paying greater attention to the daily activities and asides around our home, and to the hopes, fears, and dreams of those I love most, has paid daily dividends that are adding up to an incredibly rich life. Whether it's celebrating a loved one's victory or fighting insanity while repairing a leaky pipe, amidst the wonderment and wackiness my heart is changed for the better.

With your permission, I'd like to share some of the insights—both personal and spiritual—that I've gleaned from the fields close to home. I trust that when it's all read and done, you'll agree that home and family are gifts from God, meant to help us live our lives to the fullest.

Contents

Down-Payment Providence 1
Home Out of Range 3
Wrigley Field in My Blood 9
Close Encounters of the Presidential Kind 16
Welcome to Our Humble Commode 22
Hitting the Wall 28
Grace at Sam's Club 33
Good Riddance 35
The Two Mouseketeers 38
Lovers and Snake-handlers 43
Let's Talk 47
Sponge Brains and Prayer 49
Phoney Boloney 52
The Old Man and the Seul 56
Year of the Leap 59
Good-night, Deputy Yost 64
Secrets of the Swedish Chefs 69
Cool Beans 73
Cat on a Hot-Plate Casserole 75
My Killer Tiller 78
Night of the Cucumber Crazies 83
Down to Business 89
The Days of Whine and Road Dust 99
Lost and Found 109

Down-Payment Providence

The hunt was on: three bedrooms, four closets, five miles out of town. Add to that list a handful of other hopes for the first house Diana and I would own, and we knew prayer would be a key ingredient in our pursuit.

Truth be told, we didn't intend to buy a house when we did. But through no fault of our own, we had to move out of the house we'd been renting. So rather than continue to stuff our filing cabinet full of rent check stubs, we decided the time had come to settle down. We needed to buy a house which, on our budget, meant we needed a miracle.

A trip to the mortgage lender told us we were at least $2500 short of making the big move. That may not sound like a lot of money to you, but when you need it *now*, it's a fortune. Little did we know that God was already at work in our behalf.

"Hey, Anne!" I waved down the hall at a friend who'd dropped into my workplace on business. "Whatcha doing here?" I asked, curious as to what professional mission she might be on.

"Oh, hi, Randy," Anne greeted warmly in return. "I'm here looking for some writers for a curriculum project." She paused. "Say, you wouldn't be interested in a free-lance job, would you?"

Stunned, I could only wonder if this was indeed a miracle in the making.

We talked. The advance payment for the project would be . . . $2400.

Two days later I was asked to write two short pieces for another writing project—at $50 each.

Total: $2500.

So it's true, what God, through one of His human instruments, wanted us to grasp all along: "Your Father knows what you need before you ask him" (Matthew 6:8).

God doesn't always answer our prayers with the same lightning-quick response we experienced, but He always answers.

Take a home-buying pointer from someone who's been there: Don't even think about taking the plunge (or making *any* major decision in your life) unless you've made it a matter of prayer. You just can't afford not to.

Home Out of Range

Diana and I learned quite a lot about buying a house along the way to signing on the dotted mortgage line. By and large, owning a house has been a positive experience, although from time to time it's led us close to a negative bank account balance.

Actually, I've written elsewhere on the subject of home buying. But I have misplaced the matchbook cover on which this wisdom was penned. So lend me your ears and I will wax eloquently on the subject of buying a house. Maybe you'll pick up a tip or two worth hanging onto.

Let me begin by saying that renting is an honorable alternative to buying a house. Still, the emotional cost can be high. Diana and I rented for many years, so I write with some authority on this subject.

Renters are at high risk of developing LCDS—landlord cognitive dissonance syndrome. This condition sets in when you spot your landlord cruising out of town each weekend behind the wheel of a late model conversion van, a newly-purchased $20,000 ski boat veering from side to side behind him.

Something is not right, you say cognitively, with dissonance. *Why am I paying him to have a good time?* This is the first sign that the disorder is taking root. Buying a house is the most effective and lasting cure. The other remedy is to move back in with your parents, but at your age, and accompanied by a spouse and three children, this is sure to place a strain on your relationship with Mom and Dad.

Many obstacles await you on your quest for home ownership. In our case, having no money turned out to be a real doozie. As we learned, lenders are reluctant to proceed on the basis that you intend to make your first payment "as soon as you get a job." Your hopes are further diminished when the lending agent discovers that your greatest asset is a red, three-ring college binder.

What is needed, you are told, is a "down payment." This term derives from the overwhelming feeling of sadness that comes with not being able to scrape up the bucks needed to move forward with the purchase. You feel very *down* about this.

But there is an up side to the down payment problem. The actual amount involved is comparatively small, given the overall purchase price of today's home. Do not dwell on the fact that you'll be paying for this home a dozen or more times over.

This large sum total is on account of the interest accrued on your loan. You will have little interest in paying this interest but, believe me, it's in your best interest to do so. Otherwise a muscular-looking man wearing a set of fashionable brass knuckles may stroll up to the front door of your partially-owned home to ensure your participation in the loan repayment process. The Bible makes a disconcerting prediction about delinquency: "If you lack the means to pay, your very bed will be snatched from under you" (Proverbs 22:27). You can lose a lot of sleep if you don't fork over the cash. Besides, it's a whole lot easier to pay up than explain to your friends how you got those two black eyes.

O ur home-buying adventure began with the search for real estate, which provides a lot more equity than the fake variety.

For us, building a house was out of the question. That doesn't mean it's a bad idea for those who can afford it. Still, the more usual choice for the first-time buyer is the small, pre-owned home. Typical of this abode is the post-World War II suburban brick house, many of which reflect the stunning architectural designs of former halftrack drivers. As for Diana's and my aesthetic preferences, they were a distant second to authentic needs. Indoor plumbing was high on our list.

"So, just what price range are you thinking of?" Blanche, our real estate person asked, pulling up a chair on the opposite side of the conference table.

Right away Blanche knew any commission she earned by selling us a house would not foot the bill for a getaway to Acapulco. I credit her for not responding with one of several pointed barbs available to her, such as "Did you spend your other quarter on chewing gum?"

Understanding clearly what we could and could not afford, Blanche agreed to scout around for us. As we stood to leave, she mentioned one last item. "Now, you understand that real estate professionals work for the seller and not the buyer, don't you?" It was clear that Blanche wanted to take care of any home buying business in her office and not in court.

"Well, no, I didn't know that," I admitted. "So, who's on *my* side?"

"There are real estate lawyers," Blanche stated matter-of-factly.

Suddenly, I sensed that surviving the ordeal with more than a dime left in my pocket would become a goal second only to making the actual purchase.

True to her word, Blanche faithfully called us whenever any house close to our price range showed up on her computer listings. Dirt basement floors were common, as was thin air where we preferred a garage.

Just to be sure we were covering all the home fronts, Diana checked out the newspaper and local real estate flyers. After doing a dozen or so drive-bys, we began to see the hidden meaning behind much of real estate's upbeat jargon:

Real estate lingo	Actual meaning
"Needs TLC" (tender, loving care)	Needs top-notch licensed carpenter
"Dream home"	Only in your dreams will you be able to afford this mansion
"Charmer"	Term used to describe the salesperson trying to peddle this dive
"Won't last long"	About three months and this baby is gonna cave in
"Reduced!"	It shrank after the last flood

"Drive a little, save a lot"	What's a 600-mile commute when you can save a dime on your mortgage payment?

On site, the sign that always makes me chuckle is "Lots For Sale." Lots of *what*? Lots of nothing, it appears to me.

One day a ray of hope broke through our dark cloud of homelessness. In one of the real estate booklets, Diana spotted a "Lovely three bedroom brick rancher located in Willow Village Estates," blah-blah-blah . . . "Must see." The home was listed with another realtor, so Blanche said she'd get the key and meet us at 6:00 P.M. to give us the sales pitch.

When we stepped inside, it was apparent that the owner had gone to great expense in updating the home's interior. That was in 1962, however, and the dark paneled walls that were so popular during the Kennedy years seemed to grow closer together with each step we took.

Blanche struggled to find a selling point on which to build a credible case. "Paneling suggests that the owner was striving for a look that says 'warmth and richness.'" Opening the sales pressure valve a bit more, she added, "And at this price, warm, rich-looking homes *always* go quick."

Knock on wood, I thought, strolling briskly toward the front door. We made our escape just as the home's groovy walls were about to press us like a leaf.

It wasn't long before another house caught our interest. As usual, the dwelling was out of our price range. Still, Diana wanted to have a gander at this collection of two-by-fours. Blanche said she'd get the key and rendezvous with us at 6:00 P.M.

Another mid-60s three-bedroom brick rancher, the house had a certain appeal to us. Clipboard in hand, Blanche gave us the rundown, a word, by the way, which our hostess studiously avoided.

As we strolled from room to room it was entertaining to see this slip of a woman's biceps inflate like balloons as she attempted to deal with the several uncooperative doorknobs in the house. "These doors seem to have a little 'personality,'" she remarked, wiping perspiration from her forehead.

"Enough to host a major party," I mumbled.

As it turned out, the sellers were eager to negotiate a deal. To our amazement, a few weeks later we found ourselves attending the "settlement" proceedings, something I trusted had occurred long ago to our "new" home's foundation.

It was during these moments of parting with our money that we discovered what had happened to much of South America's rain forests. Most of it lay on the conference table in front of us in the form of legal documents. I recommend wearing a wrist support during the signing of these 10,000 or so papers, since carpal tunnel syndrome is a real possibility.

"Congratulations!" Blanche beamed broadly after the final signature had been lent. Her remark would have found more meaning had I felt it was directed toward us rather than the home's previous owners as they pocketed our life savings. Still, a celebration seemed in order. Pulling this off on the nine cents Diana and I had left between us proved to be a real challenge. But satisfied we were. God had opened His providential storehouse and poured out a magnificent blessing in our behalf. We finally had a place to call our own!

Cooler temperatures drifted our way a few weeks after we moved into our new place. As steaming-hot weather had kept us from testing the heating system prior to our purchase, we were eager to experience the warmth descending from the radiant coils located in our ceiling.

Now, you may be saying, "Why is there heat in your *ceiling?* Don't you know heat *rises?*"

Hey, don't knock it until you've tried it.

"Try knocking on the thermostat," Diana urged, shivering. I'd been trying unsuccessfully to coax some warmth from the heat system.

I rapped the thermostat, then mounted the bed and began feeling the ceiling for signs of warmth. Passersby were no doubt fascinated by the sight of a man attempting to walk across the ceiling on his hands. I followed this procedure throughout the house, my hands no warmer for their effort. The cold reality was that our heating system wasn't working!

I jumped down from the bed. "I can't believe this!" I cried, my hands momentarily frozen in the stick 'em up position.

"Better call an electrician," she urged.

Over the phone, my electrician friend, Jim, calmly guided me through a series of queries that eventually led me to a circuit breaker box on the outside of our house. Never had I rejoiced to see a tripped breaker as in that moment. I thanked Jim for his expert problem-solving, then raced into the bedroom where I stood on my head, placed my feet on the ceiling, and began defrosting my toes. Not really, but it's an idea whose time may come if the mercury dips low enough. In the meantime, we're supplementing our heating system with plenty of hugs, and making warm memories. After all, isn't that what a home is all about?

Yes, after the initial setbacks, we've settled into a routine of affection and support between family members within our home's walls. In the end, it's not square footage or elegant, curved staircases that make the perfect home. Rather, it's the love that abounds between the people who dwell therein that makes a place something special.

Did you know there's another type of house-hunting? Jesus longs to take up residence in the home of each person's heart.

"Jesus replied, 'If anyone loves me, he will obey my teaching. My Father will love him, and we will come to him and make our home with him" (John 14:23).

Have you chosen to allow heaven's power and love to move into your life? Doing so will brighten your home, and in turn the lives of family and friends. If you haven't made that choice, now is the time to say yes. You'll never regret it—you have a heavenly guarantee. Something, by the way, that accompanies a home only if you pay extra.

Wrigley Field in My Blood

The road leading from buying a house to actually establishing a home is laden with many stumbling blocks. Around our place most of them are genuine Legos, although a few generic brands have gotten mixed in. Tread this treacherous pathway in the darkness of night and you'll discover the immense pain these little six-pointed land mines can inflict upon your sole.

It all started when we began thinking about having children. Just where the idea of filling our house with kids came from is hard to say. Truth is, more than once the "spittin' image factor" threatened to quash the whole concept.

Now, I'm no expert in the field of genetics, something with which my high school biology teacher, Mr. Kesler, would fully concur. Mr. Kesler was a master lecturer, and many of his discourses involved scientific topics. But etched more deeply on my memory are his well-crafted attempts aimed at putting an end to my kneading a chaw of Bazooka bubble gum during class, or subversively talking baseball with my pal, Tom "Tomahawk" Stiles. I really liked the teacher well enough, but frankly, his field of specialty held my interest about as well as a Styrofoam nail.

I should have paid better attention. With a subject as important as the spittin' image factor at hand, it's a shame I have to rely on what few snippets I can recall from Mr. Kesler's class. Let me give it a shot.

From what I can remember, the field of genetics was first explored by the famous scientist, Gene. His single greatest discovery hailed from somewhere far out in the chromozone, and was known as "genetic matter," particles of cellular gunk with adhesive properties. Certain unpredictable parts of your ancestors' character traits affix themselves to these biological structures and are passed along. Eventually they rear their ugly heads in you and, even worse, your offspring. If you're already a parent, you know what I'm talking about. If you're just now thinking about joining the parenting ranks, the reality that your children will reflect many of your own character traits should scare you senseless. Either way, sooner or later, you're going to have to come to grips with the spittin' image factor.

Of course, any kid's existence is hardly the result of some arbitrary genetic arrangement. Each one bears the unmistakable imprint of the Master Designer Himself: "For you created my inmost being; you knit me together in my mother's womb. I praise you because I am fearfully and wonderfully made . . ." (Psalm 139:12, 14).

But the gift comes in a mighty colorful package.

Good news! There's a positive twist to the potentially negative "pass it on" side of parenting. For me, hope sprang up as memories of my own father made their way onto the playing field of my mind. . . .

I don't know if Billy's playin' today or not, do you know, Randy?" The voice of my pal, Tony Marino, drifted forward from the back seat.

"Huh . . . what?" I mumbled.

Tony glanced over at the passenger on the opposite side of the back seat, our mutual friend, Ronnie Stickley. Ronnie just rolled his eyes. I knew they could both tell that something was eating at me besides the ravenous Michigan mosquito that had slipped into the car just before I'd slammed the door shut that morning.

"I *said*," Tony repeated, "do you know if Billy Williams is playing left field today?"

"Oh. Uh, yeah, I think so."

Tony leaned over to Ronnie and I heard him whisper, "What's *wrong* with him? It's like his mind is somewhere else."

Ronnie just shrugged.

My traveling pals were right—something besides the home run hero of the Cubs' 1969 roster *was* on my mind. I was pondering when to break some really, *really* bad news to the chauffeur, who also served as my father.

"Billy *who?*" Dad chimed in.

His question came as no surprise. For some 40 years, Dad's interest in sports had been pretty much confined to the field of accounting. Enthusiasm for his preferred recreational pursuit surfaced anew around the first of each year.

"Wake up, boys!" Dad whisked back the curtains in our bedroom. "It's the first Monday of January, and you know what that means!"

"Ugh," Dave and I groaned in harmony.

"It's . . . tax season!" our father grinned.

"Oh, yeah . . ."

"Come on, boys, all together now. Let's sing!

> 'Take me out to the office,
> Take me out to my desk,
> Bring me some W-2s and pens,
> I won't be back 'til mid-April again . . .'"

We tried our best to catch the spirit of the season, but it was usually easier to catch a cold.

Dad stayed in top form by frequently working out at home. More than once Dave and I heard the sounds of our father's sporting fervency drift down to our bedroom doorway. "*Yessss!* Look at those debits and credit columns balance!"

"He's at the twenty . . . thirty . . . forty thousand dollar income level! It's a whole new ball game — and tax bracket — for Mr. Wooley!"

"I can't believe this hockey puck tried to claim his goldfish as dependents!"

Suffice it to say that Dad was not a season ticket-holder at Wrigley Field.

But April was now past, and with another satisfying tax season behind him, Dad had agreed to haul us around the bottom tip of Lake Michigan to Chicago to watch the Cubs play the San Francisco Giants. As we made our way ever closer to Wrigley's ivy-covered outfield walls, I knew there was more in store for Dad than what I'd let on.

Much more.

"There's a parking place!" Tony cried out from the back seat two hours after our departure. On the north side of Chicago, finding a parking space represented no small victory. During those years, the actual parking lot alongside Wrigley Field was spacious enough to hold two Volkswagens and a moped. The other 36,690 patrons were left to find an empty spot along the likes of Waveland or Sheffield Avenue, or pay whopping fees to local residents who in turn granted permission for fans to park twelve-deep in their driveways.

Today we were lucky, though—we found a vacant parking spot along a side street, albeit a day's journey from the nearest turnstile.

As the ornate sign hailing our arrival at Wrigley Field loomed large before our eyes, I knew the time had come to fill Dad in on the day's schedule.

"Dad," I said with trembling voice as we strolled past pennant and program-hawking vendors, "I guess I oughta tell you something."

"Sure, son, go ahead." He looked up and down both sides of the stadium for a ticket window.

"Well, I didn't want to say anything earlier, 'cause I didn't want you to say no."

Dad looked down at me. "What are you talking about?"

"I'm talking about today being a . . . double-header."

Suddenly, Dad stopped walking, and his eyes glazed over. Tony and Ronnie, who had been trailing along behind, crashed into us like dominoes.

"Hey, what are you—" Ronnie started to complain, but Dad cut him off.

"*D-doubleheader?*" my father echoed. "Isn't that *two* games?"

I swallowed hard. "Well, yeah, but it still costs the same as one," I encouraged.

"H-how many periods *is* that?"

"It's . . . eighteen *innings*, Dad. But there's some time between games."

". . . plus time between games," he repeated slowly. The whites of Dad's eyes assumed a frightening opaqueness, as if his disbelief were spilling over, running down and coating the insides of his eyeballs.

Ronnie drew up beside me. "Is your father OK? I mean, he sorta looks like he might do something awful to someone!"

I turned back to Dad. "I know I should've said something before, but I know you aren't crazy about baseball, and I—"

Dad held up his hand. "It's OK." With that, my out-of-his element accountant father strode purposefully toward the nearest ticket window. "We'll take four grandstand tickets," he spoke into the darkness of the caged window.

The woman seated inside laughed evilly. "Well, that's just what you're in for, a *grand stand*!" She hoisted a thumb toward the catwalk. "There's not a seat left in there—it's standing room only. Ha-ha!"

It was fortuitous that many steel bars stood between the woman and my father. Most people do not realize the size of biceps a man produces after pushing a pencil and punching adding machine buttons for nearly four months, 16 hours a day. Suffice it to say that this news was embraced by Dad with the same enthusiasm as if H & R Block had just rented the vacant building next to his accounting practice.

Looking over his shoulder at us three boys, we sported the most pathetic-looking facial expressions we could muster. It worked!

"Well, I guess we'll go ahead and take three . . . standing . . . room . . . only . . . tickets," Dad said. His breath came in short gasps.

But for whatever trauma had accompanied our not-so-grand entrance, at least for us boys, it quickly faded as our eyes took in the emerald-green outfield grass of Wrigley Field. Looking around, we realized the lady was right—there were more people jammed into the friendly confines that day than there were cans of peaches in Mom's pantry.

Weaving between fans, Dad finally located a couple square feet of cement near a grandstand support beam. We staked our claim, and readied ourselves for the action to begin.

To my father's misfortune, this was not soon forthcoming. Both team's pitchers were in top form that day and all the components for a truly dull game quickly fell into place. As for my own interest in the game, it mattered little that batter after batter was swatting nothing but tiny particles of dust. I was at Wrigley Field, and having the time of my life.

"Kind of a slow game, isn't it?" Tony observed during the seventh inning.

I turned to face him, and a smile of satisfaction crossed my face. "Yeah, *real* slow." Even with a conspicuous absence of line drives, as far as I was concerned, forever would be too soon for this day to end.

At the top of the ninth, Dad was pretty certain forever was long past—he was now in suspended aggravation. The score was 1-1, but that was about to change. With one out, the Giants' catcher, Joe Ferguson, homered to center field. Heading into the bottom of the inning, the Giants led 2-1.

But the Cubs mounted a rally in the bottom of the inning! With two outs, my hero, shortstop Don Kessinger, stood perched on second base, representing the tying run.

"Dad," I shouted, "this could go into extra innings!" It may have been providential to my well-being that a perfectly-thrown pick-off play at second base ended game one.

Game two proved to be more exciting. "Go, go, go!" Dad cried out when he saw four adjacent seats open up during the third inning. Deftly he swept past the distracted usher and soon we found ourselves seated in Wrigley's incredibly uncomfortable slat-back seats.

Unlike the previous game, the Cubs took a solid lead early and held onto it. Toward the end of game two, my eyes drifted down toward the box seats. I leaned over to Ronnie. "Hey, look!" I said, pointing. "Down there in the front row. Those seats are *empty!*"

I looked over at Dad, who at the moment was catching up on a few months' worth of lost sleep.

"I'm gonna try to get down there!" I informed Ronnie. Slipping out of my seat, I waited until the nearby usher was looking the other way. Row by row I worked my way forward, until I found myself staring at one of the empty seats. Plopping myself down, I settled in just as if I'd actually paid for the privilege. It turned out to be worth the risk. My heart soared along with the baseball as from my close-up vantage point I watched sweet swingin' Billy Williams drive one out of the park.

After 18 wonderful innings, I knew the time had come to head for home. Dad would be wide awake for the drive home, and probably most of the rest of the night as well. Gathering our jackets, souvenirs, and a thousand memories, we headed for the exits and made our way toward the car.

Driving down Lakeshore Drive, Dad looked warmly over at me and said with a smile, "Son, I really hope you had a good time."

I vigorously nodded my approval of the outing. The unselfishness and grace of a caring Dad had made my day.

And so it is that, years later, I know there can be more to the spittin' image factor than a future of regret. Sure, my children show evidence that they've inherited their unfair share of faulty characteristics from their dad. But I can choose to model those traits that I long for my children to lay hold of in their lives, such as the selflessness my father displayed on that long-ago day.

The best news is that, when the traits that we as parents want to pass on don't come naturally, we have a Source of hope. *Our heavenly Parent has involved Himself in our lineage!*

"And by Him we cry, 'Abba, Father.' The Spirit himself testifies with our spirit that we are God's children" (Romans 8:15, 16). *Those* genes are one-of-a-kind, and through a consistent connection with Him, their benefits can become a part of our parenting legacy.

Memories of that long-ago trip to Wrigley Field instill within me a recommitment to a parenting style rooted in grace. I trust *both* my parents rightfully consider that desire to have been inherited from them.

Our family life hardly includes a perfect model of parenting. But with God managing from the dugout, our home can increasingly become a stadium of love, a place where we as parents can applaud the victories of our children, and shed a tender tear in the midst of their defeats. We can show our precious children what it means to be parents of grace.

Sometimes that means setting the acceptable standard aside. A while back we shoved the loveseat out of the way so we could play baseball inside during a spell of cold weather (it's OK—we used a Nerf ball). I seem to have a hard time waiting until spring to get a taste of the grand old game. I guess it's in my genes or something.

Not from my Dad's side, that's for sure.

Close Encounters of the Presidential Kind

"Dad, what's whiskey?" We'd always encouraged our kids to ask questions, and now we were paying the price. The only saving grace was that our firstborn's curiosity was peaked by a historical marker rather than a genetic propensity for potent booze.

The remnants of the Blue Blazes whiskey still stands at the end of a lovely wooded foot trail within Catoctin Mountain State Park, not far from our home. We like to go traipsing through the park with our boys, exploring what someone has called "God's second book," nature. During prohibition, bootleggers headed for these same hills for less worthy reasons. I swelled with pride that my tax dollars had gone to erect a monument to those who'd broken the law so creatively. Then again, I suppose preparing oneself to make wiser choices in the future involves learning from the past. The reconstructed Blue Blazes whiskey still is 150 proof that a majority of state decision-makers agree.

Hardly an expert on the subject, I did my best to deliver a non thirst-whetting response to Tyler's question. A secondary goal was to quash any ideas my son might have about lashing a whiskey still together in our backyard to generate quick cash for Lego sets.

"Whiskey is an alcoholic drink," I explained. "It can damage your liver, shrivel your brain, and in general ruin your life." I knew that in emergency situations whiskey could be used as an antiseptic. But since we have plenty of antibacterial Band-Aids in our cupboard, I chose to let my somewhat non-subjective explanation stand.

Wandering over to the park's nature center, it wasn't long before I overheard what has to be the center's most-often asked question: "Where's Camp David from here?"

I smiled as the uniformed park employee kindly parroted the standard reply. "All I can say is that it's somewhere in the area."

What did the visitor expect? "Camp David? Oh, sure. Just head out of the parking lot, turn left and you'll see the mailbox about a mile down on the right. I'll give the Prez a call and let him know you're on your way. Watch out for those army tanks, though—the gunners have itchy trigger fingers this time of year."

Wow, I'm sure glad that park employee takes rules more seriously than those crazy moonshiners once did, I thought. *Who knows what kind of wackos would set aside all rules and common sense and try to wheel on up to the presidential retreat?*

"I think it's right through there," I whispered to Diana as we drove slowly past a heavily-wooded area, suspicious-looking barbed wire defining its borders. Not that I was actually going to try and sneak in or anything. No sir, I know Camp David is off-limits to someone like me, and I'm not one to break the rules. Well, OK, there *was* that one little incident involving the president and the Maryland state patrol and me ...

"Look, Dad, they've finished the road!" a not-so-still, small voice called out from the back seat.

I glanced out my window to the left. Sure enough, the resurfacing project we'd been driving past on our way back and forth to church for months appeared to be finished at last. Formerly twisty and pothole-patched, Mount Aetna Road had been straightened and widened. Topping off the entire project was a thick coat of shiny asphalt that now lay like a black velvet ribbon shimmering in the post-sermon sunshine. The only thing stopping us from setting our wheels on this remodeled stretch of pavement was a remaining "Road Closed" sign.

"Let's take that road home!" Tyler begged.

"Nah, it won't fit in the trunk! Ha, ha!" My witticism met with the usual period of silence, but this state of ambiance did not remain long. Pressure to travel the forbidden road continued unabated.

"Come on, Dad, we wanna see what the new road is like!"

Lecture notes on law-breaking began forming in my mind. But as I looked again at the newly-paved road, it seemed to speak to me!

What kind of legalistic, pavement party-pooper are you, anyway? the road scolded. *You're actually going to let one little Road Closed sign stop you from filling your childrens' hearts with joy? And you call yourself a father!* Then the road's attitude seemed to soften, and it cooed in a sultry voice, *Besides, no one will ever know . . .*

Hmm. Maybe the road to my left was right. I'd already slowed down, and I *could* still make the turn. *What would it be like to cruise down a road that I wasn't even supposed to be on?* I wondered. I'd done that a few times, when I'd missed my exit. But this would be different. Risky. Exciting.

It would also be against the law.

Diana showed every confidence that I'd lead my family in the right direction.

"Hang on!" I warned, yanking the steering wheel hard to the left.

Fortunately, my wife handles disappointment well. The apostle Paul's confession in Romans 7:18 had suddenly become my own: "For I have the desire to do what is good, but I cannot carry it out."

With my pulse rate on the rise, I veered around the Road Closed sign. The new pavement made our little pre-owned sedan feel as if I were commandeering a Cadillac.

"This is so cool!" Tyler said, a two-lane wide smile splashed across his face.

"Neat!" second son Andrew added in approval. Ethan, our youngest, just stared bug-eyed from where he sat strapped into his child safety seat. But I could tell we were making lasting memories for him as well. How fulfilled I felt, knowing I was meeting my children's inner needs. And all because I'd heeded the call of the unopened road. Over the smooth-as-glass pavement we traveled, beautiful South Mountain behind us, with its stretch of Appalachian Trail enfolded within its forested crest, while ahead of us was . . . *a police car!*

Suddenly my glee turned to horror. Parked smack across from the entrance to the Black Rock Golf Course sat a vehicle bearing the unmistakable tan-and-black colors of the Maryland State Patrol! Seated comfortably behind the wheel was a large uniformed gentleman just waiting to nab me!

I needed an escape route! Scanning my surroundings, I spotted my only hope of avoiding a ticket: the entrance to Black Rock Estates, the ritziest development in town. My goal was simple: to deceive the good police officer into thinking that we lived in this area, and were thereby entitled to traverse the otherwise off-limits route as "local traffic only." The odds of my family having taken up residence in one of these brick-and-stone palaces were only slightly better than our unloading a U-haul trailer at 1600 Pennsylvania Avenue in Washington, D.C., just to our south. But this time, appearances were all that mattered. If ever hypocrisy had its place, this was it!

"Hang on!" I again instructed, desperately cranking the wheel and aiming our vehicle between the two stone lions guarding the estates' graceful entrance.

"What are we *doing*, Dad?" Andrew piped up from behind me. "I wanna go home and eat!"

"Go ahead, dear," Diana spoke up. "Tell our sons what we're doing."

Explaining why our ride home from church had taken this sudden turn proved to be one of the greater challenges to my parenting skills.

Sometime later, as we cruised slowly past a 15-bedroom home for the fourteenth time, I remarked, "Just look at it, boys! Aren't those shrubs something?"

"Can we *please* go home now?"

My sons' ability to utter this plea in perfect harmony was impressive. Still, I was a little disappointed that they were showing such little appreciation for the fine aesthetics and architecture of the area. Sensing, however, that a script for *Mutiny in the Mercury* was being written in the back seat, I knew time was running out. Besides, I couldn't make too many more pass-bys before someone figured we were casing their joint for a robbery and call the police. I happened to know that it wouldn't take too long for at least one law enforcement officer to show up and begin asking embarrassing questions.

"May I see your driver's license please?"

"OK."

"It says here you live in Smithsburg."

"Uh, that's right."

"So, just what are you doing *here?*"

Oh, boy. Hi-ho, hi-ho, it's off to court I go.

It was time to leave.

"All right," I said apprehensively, "we'll head for home."

With the stealth of our car's high-class real-life cousin, the cougar, I headed toward the development's entrance. Maybe if the police officer was still on duty, the thick cloud of guilt enveloping our automobile would shield us from sight.

Arriving at the main entrance, I crept slowly out onto the road and scanned the area for the officer. Eureka! The patrol car was gone! We were home free, or at least we'd be there soon. I wiped a pond's worth of perspiration from my forehead and began contemplating how to word my prayer for forgiveness.

A couple of days later at the office I was scanning a recent newspaper, looking for info that could impact my editorial work. Closing the page, I shook my head in disgust. "That Garfield sure is a fat, lazy slug," I mumbled. Just then my eyes were drawn to a photo near the bottom of the front page. It showed the president of the United States riding in a golf cart with another man. It seems that in an uncontrollable fit of boredom, the president had drifted down from Camp David and played a round of golf at one of our local golf courses.

Black Rock Golf Course, to be specific, which is situated across from Black Rock Estates . . . on newly-paved Mount Aetna Road.

Hey, wait a minute, I thought. *When did all this happen?*

As I continued, the pieces of a giant puzzle called "Perception Meets Reality" began interlocking.

Sure enough, the date and time of the president's golf-ball getaway corresponded perfectly my family's after-church escapade. While I was sweating bullets desperately trying to pass the time of day, across the street the chief executive was having a ball slicing his way down the fairway.

Then the conscience-searing truth hit me: that state patrol officer had been posted nearby to help protect the president, not grab petty pavement trespassers!

It wasn't fair! If only I had known! Except I had. I knew that what I was doing was wrong, and if I'd chosen what was right, my anxiety level, and witness to my family, would've been much different. Instead, the words of Proverbs 28:1 were played out with precision: "The wicked flee when no one pursues."

It's a natural law that guilt puts a person on the defensive . . . and disappoints the divine.

The other night the president and I were chatting on the phone. Not to each other; he was probably resolving an international crisis while I was ordering out for pizza. But if we ever do connect in person, I'm going to tell him that next time he ought to try the golf course on the other side of town. I can't take another narrow escape from nothing.

Welcome to Our Humble Commode

One fine September day I was sprawled behind my office desk in ergonomically-incorrect fashion. As I attempted to rescue a client's manuscript from the brink of disaster, the phone rang. Dangling a participle in my left hand, I lifted the receiver and offered the greeting I'd specially honed to flaunt my professional skill and unbounded creativity.

"Howdy."

As I listened to the female caller's voice at the other end of the line, I could tell she was deeply troubled.

"We're out of water!" my wife cried.

I sensed a plumbing crisis close at hand.

"What do you mean, 'We're out of water'?"

"There's not a drop anywhere! I can't do any dishes or give the kids a bath! And the washing machine is stuck in the spin cycle!"

I expected the announcement of this much-needed break in housekeeping to be followed by mighty whoops of delight. Then I remembered that by this point in the day, a home-schooling mother of three has the energy reserves of Rip Van Winkle. Chronic fatigue syndrome is a step up. No wonder she couldn't celebrate.

"*And*," Diana added desperately, "we can't flush the toilet!"

Emergency! I had to get a handle on the situation—*now!*

"I'll be right home," I pledged.

Welcome to Our Humble Commode

A few minutes later found me testing the kitchen faucet. I turned the knob, but nothing happened. The bathtub spout furnished the same results. Snooping around the house for vital clues, I finally returned to the kitchen, where wife and kids looked at me with hopeful expressions.

"We're out of water," I reported.

That was the bad news. The good news was that I had a friend who was a plumber's apprentice. I wasn't exactly sure what this title meant, but I figured he had to know more about H^20 going AWOL than I did.

That evening, as Rick and I prepared to enter the ghastly world that exists between our home's floor joists and planet Earth, my friend spotted something unusual. Pointing to the foundation, he said, "Would you look at that!" Moving closer to the area, his eyes grew wide with fascination. "Those cement blocks are soaking wet!"

A plumbing prodigy I never claimed to be, but I was pretty certain this discovery wasn't cause for celebration.

Without further comment, Rick led the way to the plywood-covered access hole that led into our home's crawlspace. Since a valid reason to be elsewhere escaped me, Rick and I were soon sharing quality time together in what must surely be one of the most loathsome environments this side of Alpha Centauri.

Reflecting back on my experience as plumber's helper, I believe that the court system would do well to consider serving up a similar stint to hardened criminals.

Jury spokesperson: "We hereby find the defendant, Lanny Lughead, guilty on all counts."

Judge: "Mr. Lughead, you have heard the verdict. I now sentence you to accompany plumber Smith to Mr. Fishell's repulsively musty, 34-inch high, spider web-infested crawlspace."

Lughead's attorney: "Your honor! Surely you can't be—"

Judge: "Furthermore, over the course of the next nine weeks you will repeat this procedure 10 times, following plumber Smith to whatever incredibly disgusting basement or restroom facility to which he may lead you."

Lughead: "No! *Nooooooo!*"

Judge: "Finally, Mr. Lughead, in the unlikely event that you are still in your right mind after serving this sentence, you will be transported to Dendrite University, where your brain will be probed to determine precisely why the sentence failed."

Lughead (sobbing uncontrollably): "Your honor, I beg you! Give me solitary confinement or give me death; give me anything, but *please* don't send me to the pipes!"

Swift sentences such as this would have an immediate positive effect on the crime rate.

Underneath the house, Rick and I waddled about like disoriented ducklings. Finally we reached the area where the cement blocks were moist. Rick shined his flashlight overhead into the floor insulation, occasionally providing me with updates: "Mmm . . ." "Oh, boy . . ." "It doesn't look good."

On a home repair budget such as ours, these remarks hardly served as a dose of audio antidepressant.

Slowly, Rick reached up and yanked a piece of floor insulation loose. This resulted in a much-needed moment of levity, primarily on my part, since Rick was drenched in the process.

With my colleague now fully immersed in the situation, we fellowshipped together, pondering the meaning and financial ramifications of the current crisis. "You've definitely got a leak up there in the bathroom area," Rick finally said. "Let's go up top and take a look."

The invitation to exit our repugnant little well hole was received with great glee on my part. The discoveries made "up top" were not.

In the bathroom, Rick carefully scoped out the area, then strode over to the toilet stool. Wedging himself between it and the bathroom counter, he pressed his ear against the wall. Personally, if *I'd* had a sudden, overwhelming urge to eavesdrop, I would've chosen a different location. There's usually not all that much going on in our bedroom closet.

But the satisfied look that crossed Rick's face told me he'd heard plenty. "There's water running behind this wall," he announced. Straightening up, he added, "I'd say you've got a pinhole leak in a pipe back there."

Even with my limited plumbing experience, I could see the writing on the wall. I also envisioned dynamite charges and other forms of pipe bombs, and seemed to hear the voice of a salesman informing me, "I'm sorry, Mr. Fishell, but that particular tile was discontinued in 1974."

Maybe it'd be simpler just to sell the house, I thought. *We could put a sign in the front yard: "Liquidation Sale."*

"I've got a chisel in the truck." Rick's announcement pulled my wandering mind back to the plumbing nightmare at hand. "And we'll need a little piece of rubber. I'm gonna try a hose clamp on the pipe. It's a trick I've used before, and it usually works."

Strongly motivated by the idea of saving large sums of money by Rick's performing a plumber's "trick," I scrounged around in the garage until I came across a leftover strip of garage door bottom seal.

"Perfect," Rick smiled as I held out my latex offering. "Now we'd better go disconnect the toilet and move it out of the way."

"Sure," I responded. "I'm with you." Desperate men make strange pacts.

A short while later, with an assured clear distance within which to work, Rick glanced over at me sympathetically. "You wanna do it?"

I paused. "Yeah, OK." He handed me the chisel and hammer, and I began the process of defacing the wall. My initial plan was to contain the destruction within the tile's four square inch area. This approach was soon abandoned in favor of seismographically-significant blows. It is amazing how one's priorities change with the lateness of the hour.

"I'm through!" I finally cried out.

"Don't give up yet," Rick encouraged.

"No, I'm through the wall," I explained.

"Oh," he said with a nod. "Well, let me have a look."

Rick stuck his hand into the hole and felt around. Yanking it back out, it was clear that he'd struck water.

"I can't believe it!" he said in amazement. "The water's a foot deep between the studs!" Probing further, a satisfied smile crossed Rick's face. "I've found the leak," he announced. "It's just what I thought—a little pinhole job. My trick oughta work just fine."

Hope surged anew within me.

Rick dove into the job until, with a final twist of the pipe clamp's screw, the critical phase of the fix-it job was completed. As a final check, after turning the water back on, Rick ran his hand along the copper culprit. "Feels dry," he announced. "I think you're gonna be OK."

That statement turned out to be a half-truth. *I* was OK, but the toilet fixture, upon being reconnected to the water line, showed signs of severe trauma. It simply refused to go with the flow.

After a minute or so of serious reflection, Rick spoke. "Well, I guess I'd better disconnect the thing and have a look." He masked his annoyance in commendable fashion. Turning off the inlet valve, Rick unthreaded the nut and peered into the pipe. Slowly he twisted the inlet valve to OPEN, which once again, at least to my way of thinking, resulted in some of the finest entertainment I'd seen in quite a while.

"Seemths . . . ta be . . . *ptooph!* alright," Rick affirmed, swiping water from his eyes. Standing up, he sighed. "That means just one thing."

Glancing out the window at my neighbor's poolside privy, I hoped this "one thing" would not involve the quaint facility.

"Since I forgot to tell you to cover up the inlet pipe when you chipped the tile opening wider," Rick explained, "I'm afraid a piece of plaster got in there and washed on up into the toilet's float system. I'd better check it out."

"The check" told Rick that what he'd prophesied was true. "There's something in there, but I can't get it out. I'll have to go buy a new float." This he uttered with the same amount of joy associated with having one's fingernails removed by supersuction.

As Rick headed off in hopes of reaching the home improvement center before closing time, I sat alone in our bathroom-turned-war zone, pondering how this evening's events might fit into God's plan for my life. Rick, as I learned later, was very soon involved in a similar spiritual pursuit. The opportunity was afforded him by an overly-zealous patrolman bent on issuing him a traffic citation. Officer Don't-Confuse-Me-With-the-Facts was convinced that he'd lassoed the white Plymouth Horizon reported to be cruising around town busting the nighttime sound barrier. Right color, wrong car.

Later, as I listened to my dog-tired but determined friend's woeful tale, it was clear that Rick's spiritual fruit-crop of patience had fully ripened.

"Just let me know what I can do to help." This I offered in the hope that Rick's "fruit" would not enter the next stage of natural development. There's nothing worse than a plumber with a rotten attitude.

And so it was that we labored on together late into the night, Rick installing the toilet float, while I tried to think of pithy motivational proverbs on the theme of perseverance.

At last the reconnected toilet sat ready for the final test. Tense was the moment, with neither repairman daring to speak what both of us knew to be true: If the fix-it job failed, more than ever we'd need each other's support, lest one of us begin entertaining dark thoughts of sewercide.

To our great relief and overwhelming joy, the toilet, and apparently everything leading up to it, functioned perfectly. It would be some time before the same could be said of Rick and me.

As I've thought about our plumbing misadventure, it strikes me that God must feel similar frustration as He strives to correct the various malfunctions in our lives. But just like Rick, He's determined to see the job through.

"Being confident of this, that he who began a good work in you will carry it on to completion until the day of Christ Jesus" (Philippians 1:6). He's got His work cut out for Him, but the results will reflect the touch of One possessing singular skill at His trade.

Hitting the Wall

"Well, I guess I'll do it," I announced at breakfast one morning not long after the great plumbing fiasco. With my first bona fide home maintenance crisis behind me, the plumbing system was still holding its own, if you'll pardon the expression. The next logical step for me was an authentic home improvement project.

Now, the essential prerequisite for anyone embarking on such an endeavor is a firmly-rooted mistaken belief that you can actually pull the thing off and still expect your home to retain its previous value. With this perspective in place, you are ready to proceed.

Drywalling a portion of the dining room was my project of choice.

"Go ahead and hold the tape measure over there in the corner, hon." One advantage of enlisting your spouse as a coworker in such a venture is the opportunity to exchange terms of endearment on the job, something that doesn't happen all that often on your typical construction site. Your vocabulary may expand there, but not in the proper direction.

Soon the measurements we needed to forever hide our 30-year-old dining room paneling were in hand.

Home improvement tip: Cast all calculations in concrete and carry the slab with you to the project desk at your home improvement center. Do not—I repeat, *do not* attempt to recall these figures from memory! Bumps along the way jostle the numbers inside your brain, creatively rearranging them into meaningless, and soon enough tear-producing, sum totals.

My next challenge was how to move weighty and unwieldy drywall panels from the retailer to our home. The closest thing to a utility vehicle within my grasp was a little red wagon currently titled to our three-year-old son. Sure, there was the wheelbarrow sitting behind our lawn shed, but this would involve setting up water stations along Interstate 70 to prevent dehydration as I trudged the eight miles home. I didn't think the state patrol would cooperate.

Hey! I thought, *what about Joel?* I recalled that my company's staff photographer owned a pickup truck. At break time I ambled down to the darkroom and pled my case. Joel was more than happy to lend his services in hauling the drywall for me.

That evening, Joel and I rendezvoused in the home improvement center's parking lot. "So you're going to use 12-footers instead of 8-footers, huh?" he asked.

"Yep," I replied confidently. "I measured it and everything. If I run the stuff horizontally, it should come out just right."

"Bring the measurements with you?" Joel probed.

"Nah. I've got 'em up here." I tapped myself on the head. Something seemed to shift, but with Joel standing there waiting on me, I shook the weird feeling off and strolled inside. A few minutes later we were playing longshoremen at the loading dock. I helped Joel slide the goods onto his pickup's bed, and we hit the road toward home.

Back home, we off-loaded the cumbersome drywall sheets into the garage. "Thanks for the help," I told Joel when we'd finished.

"No problem." He slammed the tailgate shut. "I'd like to see the job when you're all done."

"Sure thing!" I thought of suggesting he bring along his camera, just in case he might find a use for some stock photos of an exquisitely updated dining room. But as a professional photographer, he'd likely come to see the possibilities on his own.

Since my parents were coming from Michigan to visit soon, I decided to wait and include Dad in on the grand adventure. What greater reward for a father than to witness first-hand his own offspring claim victory in a home improvement challenge? Between that and the free labor factor, I could wait a few days. For those unfamiliar with maneuvering 12-foot-long sheets of drywall into horizontal position by hand, the level of difficulty involved is about the same as pushing a loaded industrial dumpster up three flights of apartment stairs by oneself. I'd definitely need all the help I could get.

"Doing OK, there, Dad?" I asked a few days later as we trudged through the kitchen with a sheet of you-know-what.

"Y-yeah, son . . . OK." Setting the drywall down in the dining room, I noticed Dad staring wistfully out our window at the beautiful western Maryland mountain ridges in the distance. Was this a moment of deep personal reflection? Or could it be that Dad was pondering why he'd traveled 600 miles from that direction only to end up in a forced labor camp?

His thoughts remained secret, which was probably to my advantage.

"OK, let's kick it right up to the wall," I instructed. "That way I can tell how much of this baby I'm going to need to cut off."

How emblazoned on my memory are the emotions I felt during those next few moments! Suffice it to say that it is nigh to impossible to cut a 12-foot sheet of drywall and have it end up four inches longer than before, which was the amount of wall space remaining to be covered.

How can this be? I moaned inwardly. *How did the wall stretch so much without me noticing?* Then I remembered the tap on my head in the home improvement center parking lot. Never again will I try to recall construction measurements from memory, unless that memory happens to be attached to a late-model computer, and backed up in a main frame unit located in a secret underground facility somewhere in Nevada.

"Uh, I'll just tack on another piece of drywall here at the end," I proposed, looking over at Dad. He smiled and nodded knowingly. A father is sometimes required to dispense large quantities of grace when he wants to see his son claim victory in a home improvement challenge.

Soon Diana and my mom joined in the effort. Cheered on by the kids, the drywall support group hoisted the first panel into place.

"OK, just let me get a couple of screws into the thing," I said, retrieving a box of the black fasteners and my electric drill. With a *zip, zip* here and a *zip, zip* there, the sheet soon hung on the wall unaided by human hands, though its many dimples gave it the appearance of having been sprayed by endless rounds of ammo from an automatic weapon.

Soon it became clear that attaching the drywall to the studs was the easiest part of the job. Next came taping the joints, followed by the application of joint compound. Industry standard for this part of the procedure is three coats which, aside from in-between drying times, doesn't really take that long to apply. However, this was my first stab at making drywall joints come out smoother than buckled freeway pavement. I really should've accrued a decade or so of vacation time to finish the job.

After much sanding and sponging, the wall eventually sported two fresh coats of paint. To my amazement, this transformed the wall into a home improvement thing of beauty—not a single flaw was visible! Sadly, this changed drastically when I attached the chair rail molding. I can just hear some future archaeologist delivering a scholarly paper at the bi-annual meeting of the International Society of Super Scoopers:

"And to my utter astonishment, there, in what appeared to be the dining area of the home, was undeniable proof that an earthquake had indeed at one time struck the area. Undulations from massive tremors were actually still visible in the home's wall!"

OK, so it's not a perfect job, but I've got things worked out. The hutch hides the biggest wave, and nobody yet has run their hand down the wall to inspect my work. If you don't say anything, I sure won't.

As far as I'm concerned, for sheer recreational value, it's tough to beat home improvements. To reach the pinnacle, look for boxes or project instructions labeled "Easy to install." "Easy" is actually an acronym for "**e**xtremely **a**gitating and **s**tressful to **y**ou," and will furnish the most exhilaration for your money.

I only wish I'd had a video camera over the years to get some of the classics on permanent record. Such as the time my pastor, who'd worked his way through seminary as an electrician's assistant, innocently volunteered to help me install a simple, inexpensive bathroom fan. Believe me, if you want to determine the breadth and depth of a clergyperson's spiritual sincerity, just rope him into a home improvement project. I'm happy to report that Pastor Klinger passed the patience test with flying colors, though I'd give him a lesser mark in the area of physical dexterity. His ability to avoid the business end of large numbers of protruding shingle nails while balancing on a ceiling joist as he carried a variety of tools and a 50-foot loop of Romex wire rates a 6.5 at best.

Then there's the ceiling fan my lackey, er, my father and I installed in our dining room. The man from OSHA would require CPR on the spot if he knew how much weight was hanging on two not-even-close-to-code little screws.

Who knows what home improvement project will pop up next around our home? One thing's for sure, sooner or later, something will go wrong or need updating. That's the way it works (or doesn't work) in this life.

From Seattle to the eastern seaboard, I've blazed a home improvement and maintenance trail. But you know what? I've yet to lay claim to a job *perfectly* completed. Not that I haven't typically given it my best shot. It's just that, well, perfection doesn't seem to fit hand-and-glove with the human experience.

What keeps my spirits high is that my family and friends don't seem bent on embarrassing me by pointing out every quirk upon a job's completion. Nobody's called Nate the nitpicking housing inspector to see how many things he can find wrong within our home's four walls. A spirit of *grace* prevails, and celebration, not criticism, becomes the order of the day. It seems that those who love me most have more important things to do than point out the imperfections.

Maybe that's not too much different than how God views His relationship to His imperfect children. The good news is, with His amazing grace and transforming power at work in our lives, we're getting better all the time. Not perfect yet, but moving in the right direction. Theologians call this process "sanctification." I call it "heart improvements." Just ask God to fill your home and life with His power and love, and He'll fix you up.

Grace at Sam's Club

Sad but true, rule-breaking comes naturally to the human family. At times, buds on my branch of the family tree show exceptional giftedness in this area.

"Stay here, bud," I called to two-year-old Ethan as he dashed around yet another aisle end-cap in Sam's Club. We were on one of our family's spendthrift shopping sprees. You know, where with mindless abandon we whiz through the store and strip its shelves of needless luxuries such as laundry soap and diapers. With the large building's overhead lighting fixtures shedding about as much light as that of a car dashboard, keeping track of our kids was no easy task. But not to worry—Dad was on duty, giving Diana the rare opportunity to experience carefree shopping.

"Where's Ethan *now?*" my wife asked, glancing around as she hoisted a case of baby wipes into the cart.

"Don't worry," I said, surveying the area, "he's right—" But I was unable to finish my reassuring statement, for I do not possess the athletic prowess necessary to run the 100-yard dash and carry on an intelligent conversation simultaneously. Besides, the only thing on my mind at that moment was to reach the alarmed emergency exit before Ethan did.

I ran a good race, but a crown of victory was not stored up for me. Instead, I won first prize for parental irresponsibility, an achievement that was announced by the sounding of the store's alarm system. An impressive array of flashing strobe lights added to the celebration taking place in the back corner of the store. Yep, our two-year-old had scored a bulls-eye on the emergency exit handle's target.

An array of concerned store associates, along with the manager on duty, promptly arrived to size up the situation. Since there was no smoke in the area, the next logical assumption was that they'd just nailed a family of Sam's card-carrying shoplifters.

Turning to a clerk-turned-SWAT team member, I began my explanation. "My son here," I said, pointing at the little culprit, "accidentally bumped the door open." I turned in Diana's direction for support. "Isn't that right dear? *Dear?*"

Speaking to an imaginary wife during such a crisis does little to enhance one's credibility.

Thankfully, suspicion soon gave way to smiles. "It's OK," the manager said. Apparently he was convinced that an authentic criminal likely wouldn't hang around to chat with the employees. "It's not the first time this has happened," he added. With that, he instructed someone to turn off the alarm. Soon all was calm again in the southeast corner of Sam's Club. A little while later though there was quite a disturbance near the Cheerios, where I had finally located my wife.

Just in case you aren't aware of it, the tendency to do the wrong thing doesn't run in my family alone. No offense, but according to Scripture, *you've* committed your share of offenses too: "For *all* have sinned and fall short of the glory of God" (Romans 3:23, italics supplied). Thankfully, the passage doesn't end there. ". . . and are justified freely by his grace through the redemption that came by Christ Jesus" (verse 24).

Genuine love tends to furnish second chances, something of which our family had grown fond. We're back to making regular runs to Sam's Club and its sister in retail sales, Law-Mart, er, Wal-Mart. To date, we haven't had another serious brush with rule-breaking at either place. I just hope that guy I saw parking in the handicap spot and sprinting into the store learns his lesson before it's too late.

Good Riddance

The minute I walked in the house, I knew something was bugging my wife. My first clue was her frenetic welcome-home greeting.

"They're *everywhere!*" Diana cried. "In the flour, in the graham crackers, in the cookies. The little pests even got into the pancake mix!"

"Well, maybe they didn't have enough for lunch," I suggested. "After all, our three boys *are* growing children, you know."

At this juncture my wife's face assumed a look that implied my name was not on the short list for academic dean at Harvard.

"*Bugs!*" Diana said. "There are *bugs* in our food! Look!" She yanked back the cardboard flap on the Mrs. Butterworth's box. Sure enough, those weren't our kids in there.

With a fork I probed the contents of the box, then placed it on the kitchen counter.

"Can you tell what kind they are?" Diana asked.

"Buckwheat," I asserted. "But I'd sure like to know where the bugs came from."

Soon enough, my wife, who is blessed with deductive powers second only to Sherlock You-know-whodunit, had solved the mystery. "I bet they came out of that birdseed you bought last week!"

True enough, a bunch of pathetic-looking birdbrains flying around my empty backyard feeder had made me feel guilty enough to wheel down and pick up a bag of "Gourmet Mix" at the local hardware store. Upon opening the bag I'd seen a few unfamiliar, though pleasantly plump, winged things zip out. It appeared that the fare in our kitchen cupboards was the next link in the little buggers' food chain.

Just how to get these unidentified flying objectionables to buzz off became the focus of the evening. Several possibilities presented themselves, including stirring a few teaspoonfuls of Northo Bug-B-Dead into the pancake mix. I imagined this might have the added benefit of serving as a low-cost mosquito repellent for some time after breakfast. My wife, however, imagined me both hairless and demented after ingesting the concoction.

We finally decided to simply pick out the invaders by hand, then transfer the vulnerable foodstuffs to super-tight containers.

A new thought struck me. If these insects were bright enough to make their way *into* a box of pancake mix, they might have put an emergency *escape* plan in place! A briefing may have taken place days earlier:

Big Nat: OK, Itchy, if you see daylight at the top, make a break for it. You've got a good chance of getting over to the instant mashed potatoes.

Itchy: Flee, huh?

Big Nat: It's the only way, Itch. Otherwise the guy who owns this place will dump us out and try to mix it up with us!

I knew stealth and the element of surprise were critical ingredients to achieving victory.

Besides tactical preparedness, Diana and I have discovered that music can provide a boost during such a crisis. Here's an empowering set of lyrics, set to the tune of "Old MacDonald had a Farm":

> We've got brown bugs in our food,
> Yuck-yuck-yuck-yuck-yuck.
> They put me in a bad mood,
> Yuck-yuck-yuck-yuck-yuck.
> With a squish-squash here,
> And a squish-squash there,
> Here a squish, there a squash,
> Everywhere a squish-squash—
> No more brown bugs in our food,
> What luck-luck-luck-luck-luck.

Don't worry—a CD is not in the works.

It took a while, but through a long process of sealing our foodstuffs in air-tight containers, and tossing out what we felt we could replace without breaking our bank account, we eventually took back control of our cupboards. Once again we faced mealtime with confidence.

"So, kids, how do you like your pancakes?" Diana asked the boys one morning. A round of cheers brought a maternal smile to her face. The flapjacks were indeed tasty. There did seem to be a little something missing, however, and for this I was thankful.

Those bugs brought some real trouble to our home. But there's another type of invader that can reap more serious consequences than tossing out some pancake mix. Society has different names for these home-wreckers: character flaws, negative personality traits, addiction, dysfunction and datfunction. Whatever the label, their ultimate source remains the same: a very real and relentless pest called *sin*.

Someday we'll live where pests of all kinds—natural and spiritual—have been eliminated once and for all. Until then, may I suggest giving Heavenly Pest Control a call? There you'll find the Perfect solution to keeping some really serious problems under *His* control.

The Two Mouseketeers

Any seasoned homeowner knows that bugs in the cupboards are pretty near ground level on the totem pole of pest control. To truly earn one's wings requires a face-off with beasts of greater challenge. Specifically, I'm thinking of that king of the suburban jungle, the mouse.

Commonly known as the field mouse (*pastureus rodentus*), the more accurate name is house mouse (*brickus-and-vinylus rodentus*). Mice have at least enough gray matter to spend much of the year indoors. Shortly after the final game of the World Series they pack it up and head for a warmer climate.

After a long trek, the furry little migrants arrive one afternoon at their winter retreat—my home or yours—and scurry about arranging their furniture. Afterward, they collapse in a state of exhaustion, which is understandable since pushing a sofa around isn't all that easy for a mouse. Regrettably, they forget to set their alarm clocks, and end up oversleeping by several hours. Shortly before midnight they awake, refreshed and ready for a night of carousing and gluttonous kitchen revelry. This disturbing pattern of circadian confusion continues until approximately mid-April the following spring, or the moment your mousetrap springs, whichever comes first.

Scratch-scratch-scratch.

"What's that noise?" My wife sat bolt upright in bed. Semiconscious, I listened from the fetal position.

Scratch-scratch-scratch.

"What *is* it?" Diana repeated.

"Well, it's either a cat burglar sharpening his claws on our kitchen cabinetry," I groggily suggested, "or it's a mouse." This last hypothesis I uttered with less-than-overwhelming enthusiasm. My wife's attitude toward uninvited vermin is harsh. More than once I'd been sent on a midnight exterminating mission. The last thing I wanted to do right then was head off to the front lines. Maybe the tone of my response would elicit enough sympathy from my beloved to allow me to reach my goal of a good night's sleep.

Or maybe not.

Tip-toeing out to the appliance-laden battlefield, I hoped to get a fix on the whereabouts of the enemy. But to a mouse, the sound of bare feet on hardwood floors corresponds to an elephant crashing through the African jungle. Within seconds, all was silent. Yet I knew the mouse was crouched somewhere nearby, wide-eyed, and frozen with laughter that I should actually believe I could spot him.

Sometime later, having remained in a motionless state for approximately an eternity, I heard a meek though familiar scraping sound. Edging my way closer, once again the noise suddenly ceased. The cocky rodent was likely pushing buttons on his cell phone, inviting several close friends to hurry and share in the hilarity of the moment.

As for my part, I heard nothing save the irregular hum of our refrigerator. I began yet another interminable stint as a pajama-clad statue. What I intended to do with the rascal should I actually lay eyes on him remained unclear; it's not as if I was going to palm the dude or anything. But the virile varmint tracker in me was now fully awake, and I waited.

Finally the sound came again. As I listened, what to my wondering ears should I hear but the sound of little *toes*, not teeth, moving around . . . *in our stove hood*. Apparently the creature had somehow made his way into the ventwork, and little Fuzzy Astaire was tap dancing his heart out on the topside of the fan grille!

By now a familiar-looking woman had joined me. "What's he doing up *there*?" Diana asked.

"A waltz, I'd guess. But not for long."

"How are you going to get him out?"

"Don't have to," I grinned, reaching for the fan switch.

After a brief discussion, the wisdom of choosing an alternate method of destruction became clear, a mental picture having formed in my mind regarding the cleanup task *I* would soon face.

After some thought, Diana suggested, "Why not just open the grille and let the mouse drop down into a box? Then you can toss him outside . . . *far* away from the house."

Hardly the stuff of which genuine safaris are made, the idea still seemed worth a try. Grabbing a box from the garage, we positioned it on the stovetop.

"OK, dear," I whispered, "when I open the hatch and he drops down, you slam the lid shut." Diana quickly agreed to the plan, which caused me to wonder whether she was indeed fully conscious. Then I remembered the whole concept was *her* idea, which meant that even though mouse-boxing was not in our marriage vows, she'd do her part.

Slowly I reached for the latch. Diana leaned forward and lifted the box up close to the action. "On the count of three," I instructed. "One, two . . ."

"*Arrgggghhhh!*" Diana screamed, dropping the box and rocketing across the kitchen.

"*Whaaaaatttt?*" I echoed, following behind at a distance of a quarter of an inch.

"It fell on my foot!" she cried.

"*What* fell on your foot?" I panted, certain that I had yet to open the grille.

"Th—the . . ." She pointed toward the base of the stove, and we both saw it. Limp as a dish towel it lay there, which is pretty much the way you'd expect a limp dish towel to look, this one having been dislodged from the stove handle as Diana leaned against it.

Regaining our composure, the king and queen of nighttime courage plodded back to the stove for another try. With the box back in position, I flipped the plastic latch and the grille flew open.

A split-second later Diana slammed the box shut. Our eyes met, and we both knew that by pulling together during this time of trauma, we'd just sealed up a box containing nothing except two cubic feet of stale air.

With my anger now assuming meltdown proportions, I craned my neck and peered up into the fan housing. Although it was tough to see past the fan's blades, I saw just enough to explain our failed flush-out attempt. Unlike his hosts, Fuzzy appeared to be resting comfortably, having situated himself on the metal lip surrounding the stove fan. With nowhere to go but up, the little critter was unable to accomplish that feat; the vent was constructed of vertical aluminum. Since he was protected by the fan blades, I knew taking a poke at the mouse would lead to nothing but a runaround.

Now, there is a wide range of activities I would not choose to indulge in during the wee hours of any freezing February morning. Climbing a collapsible stairway into an unheated attic and disassembling stove vent ductwork would fall into this category. Nevertheless, the book of Ecclesiastes asserts that there is a time for everything, and apparently on this day 3 A.M. was the time for elevating my character. Flashlight in hand, I headed into the garage, yanked open the attic stairs and ascended to new heights.

Up top, I shined the flashlight around until I spied the vent ductwork. Like a spider taking his first steps, I gingerly moved from ceiling joist to ceiling joist until I reached the elbow connected to our stove hood. Blowing insulation away from the area, I wept briefly, since I'd just filled my eyes and nostrils with many thousand microscopic fibers.

Wiping off my glasses, I replaced them and proceeded to disassemble the joint, specifically the one I believed would provide a direct overhead view of our sleep-disturbing culprit. With a mighty yank the two vent sections separated. Lowering my head close to the opening, I shined my flashlight down into it. Staring back at me were two of the biggest eyes a tiny, terrified mouse could ever hope to possess.

Strangely, during those brief moments, the flames of compassion were stirred in this tired homeowner's heart. But only enough to make it a fair fight. Backing away, I climbed down the stairs, found a couple of two-foot long pieces of scrap wood, and nailed them together. Driven on by the vision of soon returning to a toasty bed, I crab-walked back to the scene of the face-off. Placing the sticks into the vent, I knew that Fuzzy would likely see this makeshift ladder as his only hope of escape. Whether he could muster the fortitude to bypass the baited mousetrap awaiting him at the top remained to be seen. A simple memorial service was held late the following afternoon.

Sorry, but I don't miss Fuzzy Mouse. And as God deals one-by-one with my annoying behaviors, I don't cherish their memory either. When I do think back on times when I've irritated or even mistreated someone, I realize such behavior is hardly the stuff of which heaven-bound journeys are made. Just like keeping a mouse out of my house, I want God's love and power to help fend off any tendencies toward an unloving attitude that might wish to take up residence in my soul. What an encouragement to know that "I can do everything through him who gives me strength" (Philippians 4:13).

Sometimes you just gotta call in the big guns.

Lovers and Snake-handlers

Our family has not always lived in a spacious, six-bedroom home with a Jacuzzi located just off the master bedroom. We still don't, but our brick rancher is a prime cut above the dump we once called home.

Those early days of country living were times of simplicity, solitude, and reasonable self-sufficiency. Every once in a while a good panic attack got tossed in too.

The last item on Diana's Too Much to Do list that memorable evening was a load of laundry. Burdened down with a basketful of soiled clothing, she made her way toward the basement stairway landing, crooning softly, "Oh give me a home, with a housekeeping gnome . . ." She pushed open the inside kitchen door and took one step down toward the landing. Awaiting her below was a snake who'd hung a left about a country mile too soon. Both parties nearly jumped out of their skin at this unexpected encounter.

"Yieeeeee!" Diana cried. Translated, this means, "Husband, you have exactly one and a half seconds to show your face!" This bloodcurdling scream should have at least stunned the snake. The critter, however, was audacious enough to stuck out his tongue at my wife!

Arriving on the scene, I looked down at the landing. "I see you've tossed your basketful of clothes down there next to that . . . *sssssssnake!*"

The retreat was hasty. I called an impromptu strategy session near the refrigerator.

"So," I said casually, the knocking of my knees having slowed to a lively calypso beat, "I guess you're probably wondering how *we're* going to get rid of the s-s-snake."

But Diana already had an idea. Walking over to the closet, she yanked open its door and grabbed the broom. With a sweeping gesture, she handed it to me. "You take this," she instructed. "The back door threshold is too high to push the snake outside, so I'll go upstairs and get a cardboard box." Far too soon she returned, poor man's live trap in hand. "I'll hold the box open, and you can sweep the snake into it," Diana explained. "Then we'll just haul him off . . . somewhere . . . away from here."

The finishing details to our battle plan seemed a bit sketchy, but first things first. I shouldered my virtual shotgun and readied myself for the snake attack.

As the Laurel and Hardy of herpetology, we crept gingerly back over toward the stairway and I swung the door open. "Fang" still took up residence near the baseboard. Taking the lead, I moved stealthily down toward the landing, my trusty box-toting companion following close on my heels.

"Ouch . . . *ouch!*" I snapped.

"Sorry," Diana whispered. "I didn't mean to step on your heels."

Not wanting to rattle the snake, we moved with amazing gracefulness. Our skinny intruder was likely wondering why the two humanoids nearby appeared to have been injected with large doses of a blood-thickening agent, causing them to move in slow motion.

Finally, both of us were in position, and I spoke in a barely audible voice to Diana. "OK, set the box down, then back away. I'll sweep him into it, then you slam the flaps shut."

Diana nodded her understanding of the plan. Slowly she lowered the box, its flaps spread wide open, beckoning for the snake to enter. Slowly I brought the broom over toward the serpent. With a quick flick of the bristles I whooshed the slithering idiot toward the box.

What a shot! The snake had sailed directly into the half-inch space between the box and the floor!

Although we'd never taken dance lessons, Diana and I both suddenly showed uncanny natural ability. With a one-and-a-two we pranced around the stairway landing, performing our rendition of the

Michigan Reptile Sidestep. All the while I swatted at our one-member audience. Somewhere along the way my broom providentially connected with the snake, this time with happy results. The snake was in the box, which was good, as our performance had left Diana and I out of breath.

"Good work, dear," I panted. "I'll . . . just . . . take the box outside and turn the snake loose," I said. "Get the door would you?"

"Just let me get the car keys first," my good wife replied. She turned and ran up the stairs, leaving me standing there holding the box.

"Wait a minute!" I called. "What do you need the car keys for?"

Diana reappeared, keys in hand. "You're not really thinking of letting that snake go anywhere nearby, are you?"

"Well, I thought—"

"We're taking that snake far, far away," she said with obvious determination.

"Well, OK. Just get the car door open and—"

"Dear," my wife smiled, "I'm willing to help out. But that snake is *not* getting *in* the car. I mean, if it gets loose are *you* going to stick your hand under the seat and feel around for it?"

Good point. I paused, then asked, "Well, what do you have in mind?"

A few minutes later, I imagine the following exchange occurring between our neighbors, the Stewarts.

"Whatcha looking at, hon?" Mrs. Stewart calls from the kitchen.

Mr. Stewart, a level-headed insurance salesman, sighs blissfully and replies, "Oh, I'm enjoying watching the stars—"

Just then a car comes careening wildly down the pothole-filled dirt road.

"—and Mr. Fishell holding on for dear life as he sits cross-legged on the roof of his automobile, a large cardboard box bouncing up and down in the middle of his lap."

Slowly the Stewart's kitchen faucet is turned off, and a rustling of paper is heard as Mrs. Stewart leafs through the White Pages in search of a mental health hot line.

Meanwhile, under cover of darkness, from my lofty perch I gave clear orders to my driver below. "Stop the car!"

As the vehicle slowed down, I readied myself to heave the snake—box and all—over the steep, riverside embankment off to my left.

With a mighty toss I bid my boxful of trouble farewell, then leaped from the roof and climbed inside the car. I leaned my head back against the headrest.

Diana looked over at me and smiled lovingly. "I'm proud of you, hon."

I turned and looked straight into her beautiful dark brown eyes. "I'm out of my mind."

My dear wife said nothing, which was the perfect choice of words given my attitude at that moment.

"There is a time to be silent, and a time to speak" (Ecclesiastes 3:7).

Sometimes putting Scripture into practice goes a long way toward saving a marriage.

Let's Talk

"Wenwegonahavsumlnch?
"Sure."
"Ithnkigtmypanzonbakwrd."
"Good job!"
"Mybaljuswoldintodatreet!"
"That's just fine."

What appears to be a NASA scientist establishing contact with an extraterrestrial being is actually an event of less stunning proportions. It's an excerpt from my proposed book on the vocabulary of two-year-olds. The working title is, *I Can't Understand a Word You're Saying, But I Love You Anyway.*

Admittedly, it's going to be a challenge stretching my parenting concept into a 200-page book manuscript. Let's just hope the publisher doesn't ever hear what I'm about to tell you: the way to communicate with any tongue-twisted toddler is to simply *pretend* you understand what they're saying.

I'm not sure if it's honest to offer a meaningful response to a child's sincere plea of "Juisernbbsdfllelsppdems." Just because I've done it several dozen times in one day doesn't necessarily make it right.

But really, what are a parent's options? After a couple of unsuccessful stabs at deciphering the child's language-code, it seems preferable to bring closure to the meaningless exchange rather than see it end in frustration and screaming. What kind of example are you setting when your kid sees you acting that way? Far better to furnish the impression that you've heard and understood.

You will, of course, want to drop the approach once you can actually make out intelligible sentences. The pretending-to-understand-when-you-really-don't approach can reap disastrous consequences when carried into areas other than parenting. For example, don't ever slide into automatic response mode during an important business meeting:

"Winklemeier, did you close the Seymour Optical deal yesterday like I instructed?"

"Maybe after lunch—*if* you behave."

"B-but I told you the Seymour account was your last chance to keep your job!"

"You're really special, buddy."

"Winklemeier! What's gotten into you? You're making no sense!"

"Good job! I'm so proud of you. Come here and let me give you a big hug!"

No, don't let the technique become so entrenched that it jeopardizes your being viewed as anything less than the person you are, and hopefully more.

On a more serious note, in the matter of conversing with God, phony communication won't cut it. We're admonished to foster a relationship in which we'll feel free to share our deepest concerns with our Heavenly Father.

"Do not be anxious about anything, but in everything, by prayer and petition, with thanksgiving, present your requests to God" (Philippians 4:6).

According to Scripture, the effect of establishing a clear heavenly connection is well worth the effort.

"And the peace of God, which transcends all understanding, will guard your hearts and your minds in Christ Jesus" (verse 7).

As the object of His affection, it's only sensible to carve out a slot each day for some quality chat time with the One whose "ears are attentive to [your] cry" (Psalm 34:15). It's a great feeling to *know* that you've been heard.

Sponge Brains and Prayer

Most people think that children's brains are made of the standard yucky biological stuff. Not so. Kids' skulls are filled with sponge. This allows them to soak up vast amounts of data. Occasionally they will spew forth in public the most embarrassing portions of this information, but let us not dwell on that aspect at present.

Diana and I assume that occasionally we have something of real value to add to our children's bank of knowledge. Keeping the parent/child line of communication open has been key to the process. Sometimes it all works out just like the parenting books say it's supposed to. But a while back it went something like this . . .

"Dad, what's matter?" eight-year-old Tyler asked me one evening.

"Nothing, bud. Everything OK with you?"

"Uh, dear," Diana spoke up, "I think our son is asking a scientific question."

"Feelings are hardly science," I pointed out.

"What I mean is, Tyler wants to know what *matter* consists of. Is that right, pal?"

A nodding head confirmed my wife had correctly understood.

"Oh, I get you!" I laughed. "Well, maybe when you're a bit older—" But suddenly I realized that what I had on my hands was more than a curious kid. It was a bold-faced "teachable moment"!

Diana was already on the case. "Why don't we look up 'matter' in the dictionary?" she suggested. Strolling over to the bookcase, she yanked the tome from its slot and began flipping pages. "Mango . . . matrix . . . here it is—'matter.'" She thrust the book in my direction. "Why don't you read it, dear?" One mark of a godly wife is a willingness to draw others into the circle of glory.

Bending my head close to the tiny print, I cleared my throat and began my lecture. "Son, it says here that 'matter' is from the Latin word *materia*, which means 'material, stuff or wood.' Hey, check this out!" I said, following the lines with my finger. "It says 'matter' is also connected to the word 'mother'!" Turning to Diana, I cleverly remarked, "What do you think of that, dear? Or doesn't it really *matter* to you? Ha, ha, ha!"

She urged me to return to the subject at hand.

Refocusing on the miniscule print, I went on. "OK, son, I guess here's the real answer to your question. Matter is 'what a thing is made of; constituent substance or material.'" Now that we had reached the very crux of matter's definition, I closed the volume, a smile of satisfaction on my face. I had seized and conquered a genuine teachable moment.

The parenting reward was soon mine, although translating Tyler's nearly-inaudible grunt into a cry of celebration required some effort on my part.

As he headed off toward the living room to ponder my words of wisdom, I leaned over and huged Diana. "Thanks for helping me out, hon."

Before she was able to respond, though, Tyler turned and offered a final word. "Dad?"

"Yes, son?"

"What's matter?"

I paused to reflect on this, our son's latest attempt to satisfy his insatiable thirst for knowledge. Indeed, another teachable moment was upon us, and so soon! Or, more accurately, I had spoken and, through no fault of his own, my son had not understood me. It seemed that I had spoken in terms he could not understand. I just wish I didn't do it so often. Do I have something more to learn about "getting through"?

In the end, the truth shone forth like a brilliant star in a north woods nighttime sky. Whether speaking to my son or conversing with the King of the cosmos, I needed to practice my communication skills.

Regarding the latter, there is precedence, even from One who knew the heavenly language well.

"Very early in the morning, while it was still dark, Jesus got up, left the house and went off to a solitary place, where he prayed" (Mark 1:35).

If the Son of God talked to His heavenly Father on a regular basis, can we do anything less?

I hope I've made sense of all this. Prayer is far too important a matter to be confused about. It's the lifeblood of a living connection with heaven. If that's news to you, I guess this has been a teachable moment, huh?

Phoney Boloney

During college, I took a class called "Communication Skills 101." I should've taken it earlier, say, in third grade, but recess was pretty much all-absorbing at the time. Back then successful communication skills consisted of persuading Richard Hertz to let me cut into the cafeteria line.

Butch Morowitz, another schoolmate, sure wished I'd known something about how to communicate.

Butch's dad, Mr. Morowitz, was our school principal. At one time, the man had battled polio, an ordeal which had left him wearing a leg brace and walking with an obvious limp. Oddly, this state of physical affairs seemed to, at least in one sense, increase Mr. Morowitz's effectiveness as a principal. Perhaps because he had been forced to rely on his arms more than non-handicapped persons, each of the man's biceps resembled the Rock of Gibraltar. I have vivid memories of Mr. Morowitz firing snowballs during winter recess with blinding speed and laser-like accuracy. He could also whip a softball underhanded in a manner that would've left the likes of a major-league pitcher slack-jawed in amazement. Knowing that Mr. Morowitz could easily twist any of us into the shape of a pretzel helped keep our school demeanor at exemplary levels. Nowadays, of course, students are barely intimidated by army tanks on the school grounds, since some regulation is bound to exist that prohibits its artillery from actually being loaded with anything more powerful than marshmallows.

One evening, just as I had settled in for some serious third-grade geography study, the telephone rang. *How am I supposed to study with that thing making so much noise?* I thought. But since neither Mom nor Dad were anywhere nearby, I tossed the book aside, switched off the radio, and turned down the volume on *I Love Lucy*. Lifting the telephone from its cradle, I greeted the unknown caller.

"Hello?"

"Butch . . . is this Butch?" cried a voice on the other end of the line. Immediately I recognized the caller as Mr. Morowitz.

My heart began to pound. *Why is the principal calling our house at night?* I wondered. *And why is he calling me "Butch'?* Then it occurred to me that perhaps this was a pet name by which the man was addressing me. Maybe Mr. Morowitz liked me more than some of the other students, as if I were his own son! Right then I decided to not say anything that might alter his mistaken perception of me as a responsible and likeable kid.

"Uh, yeah?" I simply said.

"Butch," his voice seemed almost panicky, "tell Mom to bring my belt to the school board meeting!"

What is he talking about? I wondered. *Why does Mr. Morowitz think we'd have his belt at our house?*

Assuming the best, I chose to believe that my principal was not in fact suffering from a minor bout with psychosis. Rather, I allowed that this nonsensical gibberish somehow held great meaning to the obviously distressed principal.

"Uh, sure, I'll tell her," I slowly replied.

"Now, you're *sure* you understand?" Mr. Morowitz reiterated. "The school board meeting is about to start, and I need my belt!"

"Uh, yeah, sure. Board meeting . . . bring the belt."

"Good. Thanks, Butch." With that, principal Morowitz hung up the phone. I meandered back over to the sofa, where critical instructions about board meetings and belts soon fell by the wayside.

It didn't stay that way forever.

Some weeks later, Mr. and Mrs. Morowitz dropped by one evening for a friendly chat with Mom and Dad. Curious to know what adults talked about during exchanges such as these, I sat in my pajamas near the top of the stairs for a little eavesdropping. It wasn't long before I almost fell out of my seat.

"Yes, the last school board meeting went fairly well . . ."

Board meeting? I remembered hearing that term recently.

". . . but I couldn't stand up to make any of my points—I didn't have my belt!"

Belt? Something definitely sounded familiar about all this.

A brief round of chortles and snickers led to a fuller explanation. "Somehow I managed to rush out of the house that night without putting my belt on," Mr. Morowitz reported sheepishly. "I called home and left a message for Helen to bring my belt to the board meeting. But would you believe Butch claims he never heard from me?"

Butch!? Suddenly a casebook study of misdirected messages began to form in my mind. Had Mr. Morowitz called *our* house by mistake?

"Yep, I hated to do it," the principal wrapped up his sordid tale, "but I had to give Butch a spanking for lying to me."

Yikes! Butch Morowitz had taken it on his innocent sitter because of what *I'd* done—rather, in this case, what I *hadn't* done! If only I'd remembered to tell Mom or Dad about the call, surely they'd have gotten to the bottom of things before Mr. Morowitz gave it to Butch's you-know-what!

Right then I knew it was up to me to clear Butch's name, regardless of the consequences.

"Excuse me," I eeked out softly, choosing to remain seated, for obvious reasons. "Mr. Morowitz, what's your phone number?"

The group of adults looked strangely at me as Mr. Morowitz shared aloud the digits in question.

Funny thing how two families that know each other can have telephone numbers containing just one different numeral.

"That's what I was afraid of," I moaned. But committed to airing the truth, I launched into my sorry story. I explained that Mr. Morowitz had actually reached *me* that evening, not his son, Butch. To my relief, as the story unfolded, mounting laughter soon gave me reason to hope that I'd climb under the covers that night minus the sting of discipline. I felt really bad that Butch had taken my punishment, but not bad enough to want to experience the same on his behalf.

I'm happy to write that Butch, who eventually joined the Air Force, has yet to circle my house in an F-16 fighter jet seeking revenge. I'm sure he realizes that human beings have a propensity for getting things confused.

God knows that too. That's why He wants us to know that, in the matter of communicating with Him, we are badly in need of help. It's thrilling to know that He has provided the means necessary to hear and respond to our prayers.

"In the same way, the Spirit helps us in our weakness. We do not know what we ought to pray for, but the Spirit himself intercedes for us with groans that words cannot express. And he who searches our hearts knows the mind of the Spirit, because the Spirit intercedes for the saints in accordance with God's will" (Romans 8:26, 27).

When prayer communication breaks down, the Holy Spirit "translates" even our most confusing messages, keeping our spiritual connection crystal clear. Amazing, but Jesus spun that possibility into reality when He, much like Butch, took the punishment someone else—you and I—deserved.

The Old Man and the Seat

"Did you have a good week?" I asked Don at church.

"Well, I guess you could say it was—" *Beeeeep!*

Our conversation was interrupted by the little electronic gizmo attached to my friend's belt. Don is an emergency medical technician, a "rescue man," as it were—rather, as he is. The little black device cutting into our exchange of pleasantries allows Don to stay tuned to a wide range of crises within our community. Once again it appeared that male bonding would have to wait. Someone obviously needed help more than I did, although some would argue that point.

Don's work vehicle is a boxy-looking step-van which, with its assortment of bells and whistles inside and out makes for an impressive looking set of wheels. Someone ought to scold the guy who did the sign painting on it, though. On the front, the word EMERGENCY is written backwards! Been that way for quite a while now. Don and the other guys have probably been too busy making rescues to take it back for a repaint.

As a parent, owning an emergency vehicle has a certain appeal to me. If I owned one, whenever a crisis arose around the house I could just hop behind the wheel, turn on the siren and lights, and speed out of town until the trouble was over.

I'm joking, of course. You won't find me running away from a genuine, good old-fashioned horrifying ordeal, as much as I might like to. The truth is, I've made a pretty good rescue or two in my time . . .

I wouldn't have even noticed the old man were it not for one of my driving tendencies, one that tends to drive my wife crazy. Quite a few years ago she noticed I have a few navigational quirks that make her nervous. Eventually she began dropping hints, the most consistent being "Would you *please* keep your eyes on the road?" I just figure with all the hype about defensive driving, someone needs to play offense. Diana thinks my driving is plenty offensive.

But this day I cruised down the highway solo, with only my good sense to help keep me on the straight and narrow. In a moment of weakness, my eyes drifted toward a house situated off to my right. Something really weird was going on. I slowed down to take a closer look. Parked in the driveway of this cottage-like house was a car whose back door was fully open. That wasn't so strange, but something else sure was. Perched on the rear seat was an elderly gentleman, apparently unconcerned or unaware that large wisps of smoke were curling out from directly beneath him! The old man was in the hot seat!

Slamming on the brakes, I whipped into the driveway and pulled up at a safe distance behind the smoldering vehicle. If it was soon to blow, I didn't want to go along for the ride.

Mustering my courage, I stepped out of my car and walked cautiously toward the elderly gentleman, who was still staring straight ahead. Apparently he didn't realize that the fuse on his skyrocket to oblivion had been lit.

What do I say without increasing the guy's chances of dying of a heart attack on the spot? I wondered. True, there was no time for a lengthy exchange of greetings. But a more basic "Excuse me, sir, but you're about to fry alive!" didn't seem to blunt the edge quite enough.

I settled for a polite salutation laced with a bit of panic. Leaning far into the rear seat area, I said, "Excuse me, but it looks like something's burning underneath your seat. May I help you out of the car?"

I arranged myself to provide assistance, fully expecting the man to express huge relief at being rescued from his pyro-predicament. That's why I was so surprised when the old guy just muttered some unintelligible response and continued staring ahead! He seemed completely unconcerned with his dire situation.

What's with this old man? I wondered, fighting the urge to lip-lash him royally for his ungrateful, not to mention foolish, attitude.

Just then the side door of the little house swung open. In it stood a large gentleman in his late 30's whose subscription to *GQ* had obviously lapsed.

"Can I do somethin' for you?" he grunted with suspicion.

"Not me, but him!" I pointed to the old man. "Something's burning underneath the back seat of that car!"

The fellow's eyes grew wide, and his shoulders jerked a couple of times. "Appears so." Then he added, "That's muh Dad sittin' out there. He can't do much by himself."

Suddenly I realized why the elderly gentleman wasn't making a run for it. His unfortunate ambulatory situation had forced him to await assistance, and he probably wasn't given to announcing his problem to total strangers. I figured father and son must've just gotten back from the grocery store or a similar jaunt, and the senior partner simply hadn't yet been helped into the house. I trusted that it would've happened sooner had the son known his father was plopped on the topside of a potential deadly disaster.

"I've got a fire extinguisher in here," the man in the doorway reported, still sounding too casual for my comfort level. Thankfully, a moment later he reappeared and headed straight over to the car. Turning his head toward me he said, "I can handle it now."

"Oh, yeah, well . . . OK," I replied uncertainly. It seemed clear that my job was considered done. Slowly I walked back to my own automobile and pulled out of the driveway. A look in the rear-view mirror told me that things were going to be OK. I just wished someone would've thanked me. But I guess that's not necessarily a part of helping to get someone out of a tough spot. In fact, sometimes the pay-off can be downright nasty.

"He was despised and rejected by men, a man of sorrows, and familiar with suffering. Like one from whom men hide their faces he was despised, and we esteemed him not" (Isaiah 53:3).

As a citizen, husband, and dad I want to reflect to my family the reality of God's gracious acts in my life and pass the joy along. Sometimes I get thanked, and sometimes I don't. But pass up an opportunity to help someone out of a tough spot or brighten their day just because they might not express appreciation?

No thanks.

Year of the Leap

The year 1947 is special to me, even though its days sped by without me noticing. It's hard to remember much when the very concept of you has yet to be thought of.

About this time, a man whom I shall call Dad had just completed a stint in the U.S. army. Stepping down from a Greyhound bus in his hometown of Allegan, Michigan, he strolled inside the station. There he noticed a petite young lady, whom I would one day affectionately refer to as Mom. She was in the process of closing up the soda fountain for the evening. The returning soldier's heart skipped a beat or two, then he plucked up the fortitude to speak to the lass. Soon the two were engaged in deep conversation, and not long thereafter were engaged to be married—on June 18, 1947, to be specific.

But something else was going on that year. On the other side of the state, a tractor was being built in a factory owned and operated by the descendants of Henry Ford. Neither the workers putting the parts in place nor those applying the shiny gray and red enamel to the tractor knew who would eventually own this fine piece of farm machinery. Joe the Fender Bender didn't say, "Gotta make this one extra-special—someday that soldier who just got married is going to own it."

But two decades later that's what happened. Dad, who had by then established himself as a certified public accountant, could never quite rid himself of his love for manual labor. So he bought the farm—20 acres of run-down fruit trees, two shacks that former hired laborers had called home, and a barn that was a dream come true for us two boys. The only thing missing was a tractor, and it stayed that way for quite a few years. But the day finally came when Dad came putt-putting into the driveway, perched proudly atop his newly-purchased, although by now rather old, 1947 Ford tractor.

Later, as it sat in all its pre-owned glory near the east side of the barn, a great wave of desire washed over me. At 12 years of age, I was ready to ride. Indeed, not merely ride it, but lay hold of its well-worn steering wheel and place its gearshift knob into forward. Working to my advantage was the fact that, in those days, pretty much no one outside of Washington, D.C., had heard of child safety concerns. So eventually Mom and Dad agreed that my 15-year-old brother, Dave, and I could learn what we needed to know to help out with our family's growing concerns. While Dad was balancing books and Mom was turning our old house into a home, Dave and I would be tearin' it up on the tractor!

Finally my big day arrived. "Now remember," Dad urged, "these two pedals are the brakes. You've ridden with me quite a few times now, so you know how to use them and the other levers and pedals, right?"

I nodded my understanding. Although the tractor seat was hardly form-fitting to my small sitter, at long last I was in a position to drive something that didn't require my legs to propel it.

"All right," Dad stated, "I guess everything's ready. I'll just climb up and ride along."

This last twist hardly lent itself to the image I'd formed of myself as the Mario Andretti of the vegetable patch. How would I ever gain pole position for the Indian Corn 500 with an extra passenger weighing me down? Only later, as a father myself, did I come to appreciate the Hop-a-long Daddy concept. You've gotta make sure the kid's ready before you cut him loose.

Standing on the rear axle and leaning against the fender, Dad pointed toward the starter button. "Fire it up," he instructed. I reached down and pushed hard on the little round device. The old tractor's engine turned over a couple of times, then roared to life. My heart rate soared.

"Give it a little gas," Dad shouted, pointing to the throttle control.

Reaching out, I pulled the lever down about halfway. No corporate executive ever felt the sense of power I did at that moment.

"You remember what to do?" Dad called out.

With a confident nod I set the tractor, and the wheels of adolescent progress, in motion.

I don't remember many details concerning that monumental ride of passage, or the first time I whipped around one of our property's various weed patches solo. But those early forays must have gone OK, because it wasn't long before I was pulling plowshares and performing other daring feats of farming. I was getting so good at driving the tractor that I really wished I had an audience. What good was it being the world's greatest kid-cultivator if no one besides your family ever lay witness to your abilities?

One day in June I got the chance to show my stuff. Mom and Dad were caught between dropping bean seeds into neat furrows in one end of our huge garden and carrying on a decent conversation with their furloughed missionary friends, Mr. and Mrs. Wilcox, who had dropped by for a friendly visit. To my fertile mind, this was the moment I'd longed for.

Sauntering over to the old tractor, I mounted it and pushed the starter button. Moments later I was doing a slow warm-up lap in the still-unplanted section of the garden. I knew, of course, that such lackluster maneuvering would hardly send the Wilcoxes back to the mission field with a tractor-driving tale worth telling. Luckily for them, I was readying myself for the "big one."

Casually I jounced along toward the south end of the garden. My plan was to line up for one grand, wind-in-my-face shot down the entire length of the garden. No plowing, no discing—just sheer speed, the sight of which could only leave our visitors breathless and in awe.

All was nearly ready. Wanting to gain perfect alignment for my memorable dash, I shifted the tractor into reverse, then pushed the stick in the direction of first gear. I fully expected the tractor to change course accordingly. But I quickly discovered that my expectations were not being realized. The tractor wouldn't go into first gear! I stood up, one foot on each brake pedal. No luck—the tractor was still moving backward, in terrifying jerks, toward the slope behind me. My plan was going downhill fast!

About this time Dad heard in the distance his beloved farm machine sounding as if it were suffering a multi-cylinder seizure. He knew something was amiss. Glancing up, my father spotted his fame-seeking son bouncing up and down on the tractor seat like a greenhorn wrangler atop his first bucking bronco.

The latent Olympian within my father was suddenly fully awake. With the speed of a Jesse Owens, and determination to match, Dad zoomed seemingly airborne over sprouting radishes and peas, his only goal a major rescue. One thing I knew he didn't want to plant in the ground that day was me.

Almost before I knew it, Dad arrived and leaped on the tractor. With a deft move he shoved his foot down hard on the one pedal I'd neglected to try: the clutch. Immediately the tractor's horrifying convulsions came to a halt.

Dad looked over at me, and with great zeal shared his conviction that I seemed to have left my brains inside the house. His next command was to head that direction and make every attempt to find their whereabouts.

Mom managed to regain her speech a few minutes later. As for my brother, Dave, he was probably locking and barring his bedroom door in abject fear of his crazed sibling now strolling in shame and regret in his direction.

One thing was for sure: the Wilcoxes would have a story to tell to the nations.

Actually, I've experienced more than one earthly rescue. Years ago, a bowl of grits almost did me in. Fortunately, perhaps providentially, my buddy Dwight was standing next to me in the kitchen as I tossed a spoonful of the starchy stuff down my wrong throat. When he noticed that I was unable to suck in air, Dwight politely yet firmly performed the famed Heimlich maneuver on me. I breathed a great sigh of relief.

My mother tells of the time when, at around the age of two, I managed to discover the stash of butterscotch candy she'd tried to hide from her sweet-toothed toddler. The story goes that a few minutes after I'd popped one of the candies into my mouth, I began changing color like a traffic light. To hear Mom's version of the incident, by the time she'd whisked me out to the car to rush me to the doctor, blood was rushing out my ears. Right about then the butterscotch ball must've shrunk to manageable size, because it dislodged itself. But let me tell you, that time Mom was knee-deep in a rescue of legendary proportions.

On the spiritual side, whether it's our own clan or the extended family of God, there is none who has not stood in need of rescue. Without it, the war is over, and the enemy has won.

But a Redeemer arrived to save us from an otherwise inevitable defeat.

"Who will rescue me from this body of death? Thanks be to God—through Jesus Christ our Lord!" (Romans 7:24, 25).

Like a devoted parent rushing to the aid of a child in distress, heaven's hope of rescue had arrived in human form. And just what is the upshot of falling head-over-heels into the arms of Jesus?

"Therefore, there is now no condemnation for those who are in Christ Jesus . . . in all things we are more than conquerers through him who loved us" (Romans 8:1, 37).

In this life there are no guarantees that earthly rescue attempts will end in success. Not so with Jesus. Choose Him as your rescuer, and someday we'll swap stories of how He saved us from sin—and ourselves—by His amazing grace.

Good-night, Deputy Yost

"Guess I'd better head out for the church board meeting," I announced, sliding back my chair from the supper table. I hardly consider such occasions a night out with the guys, but it's nice to know others think I might have something to say worth listening to.

As I zipped up my jacket, Diana smiled.

"What, do I have it on inside out or something?" I asked.

"No, I was just thinking back."

"About what?"

"Well, the first time we ever hired a baby-sitter was on a board meeting night, remember?"

I paused. "Uh, yeah. I remember." I kissed Diana good-bye, waved to the kids, and headed toward the garage.

Do I remember? I thought as I pulled out the driveway. How could I possibly *forget* that night when good intentions and youthful aspiration collided with reality? . . .

"And so, friends," my new boss and senior pastor proudly announced, "let us give our full attention to our new youth pastor. Turning to me he said, "Randy, please share with us your hopes and dreams for the future."

"Thank you, Pastor," I began. Pausing for dramatic effect, my next words were aimed at emblazoning on the board members' minds my philosophy of youth ministry.

"Friends, I am convinced that today's youth must be guided to where they are going, and as their leader it is I who must go where they are being led." Well, it was *something* gripping like that.

Board members cast sideways glances and whispered to each other. Clearly my words were making a deep impression. Energized by their reaction, I launched full-speed ahead into my discourse on how this recent seminary graduate would forever transform the face of youth ministry in their church.

The ministry plan I shared that evening met with absolutely no resistance, save the one person who was still awake when I finished. He made it clear that results were of much higher priority to him than platitudes. It didn't take a seminary dean to tell me things hadn't gone too well. But as the well-known psychiatrist Dr. Victor Frankl once said, "That which does not destroy me makes me stronger." I discovered that a person can get pretty sore in the process, however.

After the closing prayer, I picked up a sliver of my ego from the floor and found Diana, who had been busy elsewhere in the church during the meeting. On the way home I shared a few snippets of the memorable session. "Well," she consoled me as we pulled into the driveway, "when we get home, we'll just leave our troubles outside."

But back home, it was clear that carrying out this order wouldn't be easy. Opening the front door, our ears were blasted with a high-pitched wailing sound.

"I tried everything to get the baby to stop crying," Jodie, our baby-sitter fervently apologized. The distraught girl's anguish was almost as great as that of her two-month-old client's. "It's just that I didn't want to bother you while you were away . . ."

"It's OK, Jodie," Diana comforted. "I didn't know his separation anxiety would be this intense." She turned to me. "Dear, would you please pay Jodie?"

I pulled out my wallet and reimbursed the girl for her evening from you-know-where. Meanwhile, Diana headed off to the nursery with our little bundle of neurosis. Moments later the child was sawing logs like the best of them in the Pacific Northwest.

Back in the present, I shook my head as I continued my trek down Maryland route 66 toward the church. *Separation anxiety!* I chuckled to myself. *Why, somebody was right there with him the whole time!*

Where in the world did this kid come up with that kind of insecurity? It's not like I fell apart every time my folks left me with a baby-sitter.

But then again, perhaps my musings were a bit on the selective side. Sheepishly, I had to admit that I, too, had experienced my own childhood night of terror . . .

"It was *real!*" I sobbed my seven-year-old heart out to Charlene, our teenage neighbor and my baby-sitter for the evening. She gently patted my back, probably hoping this might jar loose some biological shut-off valve and lower my fear level. At the same time she peered up into the insulation of my half-remodeled bedroom. "So, Randy, you're saying that you saw something move up there, is that right?"

I sniffed again, and nodded.

This event was before the days of baby-sitting workshops, where today's hopefuls learn emergency lifesaving techniques and gain legal counsel on how to sue for damages should they trip over a misplaced binkie. Charlene had no training in how to respond to a sittee's claim of having seen a human hand protruding from between his bedroom ceiling joists.

"I really don't think there's anybody up—" she began.

"When are Mom and Dad coming back?" I eeked out between sobs.

"Well, their meeting isn't over quite yet," Charlene explained. But even her best efforts to calm my anxiety weren't working. The cold reality was that four long miles of highway separated me from my earthly source of security.

Between my tears I saw Charlene make her way over toward the bedroom doorway. "I'll be right back. I need to go call my dad at home."

Her dad?! Mr. Yost was a big, strapping deputy with the county sheriff's department! Was Charlene going to tell him to tote his billy club and .38 revolver up to persuade me of the virtues of dropping quickly off to sleep?

In retrospect, I can envision the joy with which Charlene's call was received, the man's daughter having interrupted both his evening off and the second half of a particularly gripping episode of *Gunsmoke*.

"Hello . . . *Look out—behind you, Festus!*"

"Hello, Dad? This is Char." "Yes, I know you really like Matt Dillon, Dad." "Yes, Dad, you've told me about Boot Hill."

After a few more reprimands and reminders, Charlene continued. "Well, Dad, the boy's having a little trouble getting to sleep." She went on to explain what I had reported as having seen overhead in my bedroom ceiling. "So, well, Dad, I was wondering if you could . . ."

I couldn't bear to hear the rest. Diving under my pillow, I drew it up tight to my ears. With all my might I hoped Charlene's plotting wouldn't find me sharing a plot with Dastardly Not-Quick-Enough-to-the-Draw Dan in Boot Hill Cemetery.

A moment later, Charlene reappeared in the bedroom. "Randy," she smiled, "come over here to the window with me, would you?"

Slowly, uncertainly, I obeyed. Was she setting up the target?

"Look down the road toward my house, OK?" the girl instructed.

Craning my neck, I peered into the night. Far down the road a police cruiser was turning out of Charlene's driveway! "Ohh noo . . ." I cried, beginning to tremble.

"It's OK," Charlene soothed. "Just watch."

So I did, and my worst fears continued to materialize. The police car stopped smack in front of our house! Suddenly, the cruiser's floodlight snapped on, and the Fishell farmstead was bathed in sun-like brilliance. With a back and forth sweeping motion the spotlight's beam lit up every nook and cranny of our house, barn, and a few other deteriorating farm structures.

And then I realized what was going on. If anything—or *anyone*—were creeping around our property, they'd be caught red-handed in the beam of the patrol car's spotlight. Charlene had asked her Dad to come up to help soothe my unfounded fears, not create more of them!

Just then the cruiser's interior light flicked on and the vehicle's window rolled down. "That enough, Char?" Mr. Yost's gravelly voice boomed into the night.

His daughter looked at me, where she saw a little smile playing at the corners of my mouth. "Yes, I think that ought to do it, Dad," she shouted back through the screened window. "Thanks."

"OK." He paused, then added, "You can go to sleep now, Randy." Mr. Yost shook his head and appeared to chuckle more than once. Then he switched off the spotlight and rolled his window back up.

Backing into our driveway to turn around, I watched with admiration as this gentle giant of a sheriff's deputy headed back toward Dodge City, er, home.

Charlene turned to me. "He's right, you know," she said, "you *can* go to sleep now. There's absolutely nothing to be afraid of."

"OK," I said, and slid back under the covers. Thanks to this caring, competent baby-sitter who'd gone beyond the call of duty, I finally felt safe. "But leave the hall light on, alright?"

"Sure," said Charlene.

* * *

Pulling into our church's parking lot, I had to admit that I'd slipped into "fear gear" more than once in my life. And, honestly, sometimes I still do. Those are the times when I try to remember this classic crisis-crusher from the Bible: "So do not fear, for I am with you; do not be dismayed, for I am your God, I will strengthen you and help you; I will uphold you with my righteous right hand" (Isaiah 41:10).

Life without God? Now *that's* a scary thought.

Secrets of the Swedish Chefs

"What's for supper?"

Around our home, that question pops up at virtually the same time each day. It is the third section of the mystic chant known as the "Metabolic Mantra." The other two phrases are "What's for breakfast?" and "What's for lunch?"

Food has always been a big part of our boys' diets. They've tried other things, from coins to sandbox sand to whitewall tire cleaner. Ethan once tried a swig of Miracle-Gro. I suppose he'd grown tired of always looking up to his older brothers. Ethan was OK, but it seems to me that for a while there we were making an awful lot of trips to barber Pete's establishment.

If this type of thing keeps up, our kids' forays into the world of non-edible foodstuffs will surely bond us with the folks down at a certain emergency service.

"Hello, poison control."

"Hi, Beatrice, this is—"

"Well, howdy there, Mr. Fishell! Haven't heard from you since last Thursday! How're the boys? Oh, but there I go again. Now, what did they get into this time?"

Maybe it'll turn into a witnessing opportunity.

So far, our sons' definition of meaningful nutrition is in question. Cartoon character-shaped macaroni with its 100% non-natural florescent orange cheese is considered a delicacy. Throw in a hard-boiled egg and tastebud nirvana has been reached.

Diana's Swedish lineage has helped to broaden my gastric horizons. Early on, some of the traditional family recipes seemed odder than a four-legged ludefisk. My first exposure to Swedish fare was *krups* (pronounced "krips," more or less), a shortened version of *krupkokker*, which holds no meaning to me either.

The story of krups' origin is hazy. As with the development of any dish worth its salt, early efforts were hit-and-miss. One version (mine) of the very first attempt goes like this . . .

After a morning of strenuous hoeing in the north field, Olaf Gunderson ambled back to the house for lunch. The famished farmer sat down at the table while his wife Ingrid scooped something from a steaming pot and placed it in a bowl. Smiling sweetly, Ingrid said, "I call my new recipe *krups*."

Olaf gave thanks for the food, ate his krups without comment, and prepared to return to the field. Upon opening the door, he was surprised to see that his fellow farmer and neighbor, Sigurd Lutherson, had just arrived for a friendly visit. Immediately a look of concern crossed Sigurd's face. "Oolaf, friend, new oofense, but you look a bit like death warmed oover!"

Clutching his stomach, Olaf replied in short gasps, "It's my wife's new recipe! Sigurd, friend, I sense I may not live to see the rising of tomorrow's sun. Truth is, if I were rich enough to own one, I'd tell you to prepare my crypt right now!"

Inside, Ingrid had neared the door just in time to hear Olaf utter these last few words. *Did Oolaf say to Sigurd, 'Prepare my krup right now?' So Oolaf liked them and he wants Sigurd to make another one for him!* Ingrid was delighted, though deluded, about her husband's appraisal of her new victuals. She then thought, *Sigurd need not bear this burden. I'll make krups again for supper!*

And so it was that a second helping of krups was served. Through the years the recipe was shared and refined, resulting in the dish we know today.

The main ingredient in the kruptic Swedish recipe is that rare delicacy known as the potato. Soon after marriage I discovered that the old country's motto of "If it can be made, it can be made with potatoes" lives on in the immigrant's descendants. Neighboring Denmark has

Legoland, but rumor has it that plans are underway for a Mr. Potato Head theme park near Stockholm.

In the matter of krup-making, physical conditioning is imperative, since you will be turning a meat grinder's crank until your right or left arm falls off, whichever leaves first.

Vocal training is a good idea as well. Without it, you may lose your ability to urge on your offspring during the last critical moments of potato-smooshing. You could, I suppose, pull the army cot on which you lay recovering over closer to the action and whisper loudly, but only as a last resort.

As for the actual krup, each one consists of a cup or so of ground potatoes, flour, and onions molded into a snowball shape. Next a section of hot dog is inserted into the starchy mass. Being vegetarians, our family's "hot dogs" consist of a soy-based meat product, which, as I write of it, makes the whole arrangement seem even more bizarre. Finally, each loaded krup is dropped into a large aluminum pot filled with boiling water laced with bay leaves and allspice. There the little spudballs will cook until Swedish intuition says it's time to eat.

On the plate, it's important to top-dress your krup with butter or margarine. The actual amount may vary from about a half-teaspoon to a front-end loader bucketful. Grab the saltshaker and let the accolades begin.

I proudly admit that I join the festivities with great zeal. It took a few family gatherings to train my taste buds to appreciate krups, but nowadays I'm ready when they are. My joy approaches ecstasy if I happen to have beaten the odds and ended up with the "special" krup, the one into which my playful wife has inserted not one, but *two* pieces of hot dog! Hitting the double weenie is a thrill beyond words.

Potato sausage is another extended family favorite. Make these by preparing a pile of spuds per standard grinding procedure. Next toss in some ground beef, spices, and whatever else goes into the concoction (I've never had the courage to ask for a complete listing of ingredients). Grab a funnel and begin shoving handfuls of this mixture into the "casing," a culinary-correct term for a cow's intestine. If there is any saving grace in the whole matter it is the fact that the intestine has at least been removed from its previous owner. Finally, tie it off and twist the three-foot long sausage around in a shallow baking pan and allow it to stew in its juices until all memory of its origins are forgotten.

OK, so maybe I've been known to indulge in the veggie version of this one too. I'm not sure, though, where stuffing soybeans inside a cow's intestine falls on the scale of commitment to a vegetarian diet. Matthew 15:11 offers me a little comfort: "What goes into a man's mouth does not make him 'unclean,' but what comes out of his mouth, that is what makes him 'unclean.'"

Still, when I think about the ethics of my practice, I wonder if words from James 1:8, though wrested from their immediate context, are more fitting: ". . . he is a double-minded man."

I don't have time to talk theology right now, though. I hear a commotion out in the driveway. It might be the shipment of butter I ordered, and I need to tell them where to park the front-end loader.

Cool Beans

My personal journey over food's hill led me to adopt a lacto-ovo vegetarian diet. Aside from the occasional potato sausage casing (which, by the way, I do not actually devour; the good stuff is scraped cleanly out), the closest thing to meat in my diet is a T-bean steak. No, God doesn't love veggie-heads more than Jimmy Dean or Swedish cooks or anybody else. Diana and I just happen to think Genesis 1:29 points in a positive dietary direction: "I give you every seed-bearing plant on the face of the earth and every tree that has fruit with seed in it. They will be yours for food." We figure the Head Dietician must've had a good reason for not prescribing an original menu requiring the services of a butcher shop.

Come and listen to my story 'bout how we stay fed.

Although Diana has been a lifelong vegetarian, I was a young adult when I made my meat-deleting decision. This was more courageous than it first appears. Back then, locating vegetarian fare at a fast food restaurant was about as easy as finding fat calories in a celery stick. Thankfully, now, largely due to the growing acceptance of such delights as the bean burrito, my years of searching in vain for meatless quick cuisine are over. I can wheel up to the drive-through just like one of the regulars. You can't really grasp the sense of normalcy this brings unless you've spent many years ordering quarter-pounders "minus the meat," a selection that frequently left the person taking the order confused and stuttering. Over the years, we've learned a few things about vegetarian cuisine. Just in case you're considering a non-meat diet, here are a few tips.

Embrace the selfless soybean. One of the staple products for vegetarians is the soybean. In the field of non-meat protein, the soybean stands alone. This illustrious legume is to the vegetarian food industry what duct tape is to do-it-yourselfers—its uses are virtually endless. The soybean has given itself over to being whipped, pressed down, and mashed into an astonishing variety of meatlike products, many of them edible. Don't worry—whether your food personality is sangwine, melancoffee, phlegmeatic, or caloric, you'll find something to tickle your changing tastebuds.

Since its inception, producers have tried to make their products appear and taste like the real thing. The goal is to help smooth the transition from meat to healthier alternatives. Accordingly, these food items are sometimes referred to as *weaners,* though not too often.

Be wise and beware at potlucks.

"This combination is absolutely scrumptious!"

"Why, thank you! I got the recipe from the cookbook, *Soybean Surprises and Duct Tape Stews*."

Should you overhear such an after-church exchange, you'll probably want to avoid the dish under discussion, including what's in it. That is, of course, unless it's already too late, by which time you'll feel as if your intestinal tract has recently been repaired by a do-it-yourselfer. Fortunately, from personal experience I can tell you that the typical vegetarian potluck is far more a tastebud utopia than a laboratory for sinister soybean experiments.

Someday my kids will have to make their own decisions about what kind of diet they think is best. Diana and I have made ours for life. We think going meatless helps keep the Holy Spirit's temple, our bodies, tuned up. Call it preventive maintenance.

Who knows? Maybe we'll see *you* in the produce section sometime, where we'll have a chance to not meat.

Cat on a Hot-Plate Casserole

Family, friends, and food just seem to go naturally together. Toss a tactless feline into the mealtime mix, however, and you've got a course of another color.

"Randy, Diana, this is LuEllen," our longtime friend Jim introduced his date. Jim was single, and Diana and I were still kidless, and the evening held great promise for strengthening the bonds of friendship without interruption.

Following the formalities, Diana sported her most hospitable smile and announced, "Well, you two are just in time. Supper's ready and waiting on the dining room table."

At the time, our childless abode was home to a colorful assortment of critters, including a former vagabond cat we'd named Tigger. With its dozen or so personality quirks, this wacky furball would have benefited greatly from a few sessions with a good clinical psychologist. Without a doubt the most irritating of his dysfunctions was his preference for sucking on an article of clothing, the main requirement being that someone be wearing it. We figured mama cat must've been hauled off by animal control before she'd fully weaned her offspring. But on our budget, cat therapy was about as likely as announcing to Jim and LuEllen that they'd need to eat quickly if we were going to get our after-dinner yacht cruise in.

I pointed to the two chairs on the opposite side of the table. "Jim, why don't you and LuEllen sit right over there?" Soon we were all seated, ready and waiting to chow down—er, partake of the fine dinner

Diana had prepared. And tonight's meal was no cardboard container cuisine. After all, we owed it to Jim to let any potential betrothed know that, despite the cracked plaster and vintage carpeting suggesting otherwise, her date was friend to a real high-class couple.

"OK, if everyone's ready, let's pray." With heads bowed reverently, I began. "We thank you, Lord, for this wonderful meal and the good friends with which to—"

Thunk!

"—Amen."

Opening my eyes, I could tell right away that LuEllen had not anticipated that live cat would be on the dinner menu. But there he was—Tigger, sitting smack in the middle of our exquisitely-arranged table, having pounced upon it during the blessing like one of his ancient ancestors. He seemed uncertain as to whether to go for the casserole or start with the tossed salad. I prayed earnestly that his affection for 100% cotton blouses would not add to the disgrace of the moment.

As for LuEllen, she was considering dashing boldly through the front door, with or without it being open.

"I, uh, Tigger . . ." I stammered, trying to find the right words with which to address the situation. Had a dictionary been handy, Diana would have been locating the word "mortification," just to be sure that this was indeed what she was experiencing.

Quickly leaning over to remove our uninvited dinner guest, I tried to recall whether I'd ever learned of a right or wrong way to displace a mangy cat who's suddenly materialized alongside a dish of mixed vegetables. In the heat of the moment, I reasoned that *how* the task was accomplished was less important than that it happen quickly. Displaying the lightning-like moves of a master illusionist, I soon had Tigger off the table.

Fortunately, no sooner had the deed been done than hearty outbursts of laughter filled the room. Jim's irrepressible sense of humor rubbed off on LuEllen, along with quite a few cat hairs. What seemed destined to destroy everyone's evening ended up serving as an icebreaker to a round-table discussion of a wide range of zany tales, punctuated by clanking silverware.

Jim eventually ended up exchanging addresses with LuEllen, though not wedding vows. She probably figured marriage is challenging enough without getting together with someone whose circle of friends included us.

As for Tigger, for quite a few days after he regained consciousness he made it clear that he was considering ending our relationship.

These days I think a lot about food, and those who don't have much of it. In an age of widespread hunger and famine, sharing lighthearted stories about food seems almost in poor taste.

In our home, I try to help keep us aware that, except for the grace of God, the tables could be turned, as it were. It could be *us* awaiting a handout for our family in some impoverished country. So before each meal, we strive to give sincere thanks for what God has given us. Maybe not enough thanks, but we do know that we're blessed as relatively few in this world are. It's our calling and privilege to pass the goodness on whenever we can.

Someday, God's faithful family will share a great meal together around what will be a very large table. (Don't worry—it'll be good and solid, built by a Master Craftsman.) In Revelation 19:9, John the Revelator, following angelic orders, extends the invitation to this special occasion:

> **Blessed are those who are invited to**
> **the wedding supper**
> **of the Lamb!**

Don't choose to miss out on this meal. Just thinking about you not being there sorta makes me lose my appetite.

My Killer Tiller

7:45 A.M. The adrenaline surged like a tsunamis wave. Thinking about garage sales does that to some of us.

But first things first.

I pulled the car up to our bank's automatic teller machine. Turning to my bargain-hunting accomplice, I asked, "How much money do you think we oughta get?" It's fun to talk like that, as if our bank account held limitless reserves. Call it a cheap thrill.

Diana's mental calculator kicked in, tabulating the funds she figured we'd need for that week's quota of the three "g's": groceries, gasoline, and garage sales. "Forty-five dollars," she finally replied confidently.

I stared back, bewildered. *Why doesn't she just round it off?* I wondered. *If it were me, I'd get $40 or $50.* I couldn't figure out the logic behind Diana's mid-range money suggestion.

But then it hit me. My wife was exhibiting classic symptoms associated with female specificity disorder. This tragic problem is rooted in an insatiable need for details. The disorder involves a malfunction of the gland responsible for allowing an individual to speak and act in broad, sweeping terms.

Whereas I prefer to deal in generalities ("I got the thing for about fifteen bucks"), Diana considers it a breach of ethics to not provide full disclosure in similar instances ("The 24-ounce bottle of Grit-B-Gone was $3.27 at Sampson's, but last Tuesday evening I found it on special at Countryside Market—in aisle 9-A—for $2.76, plus sixteen cents tax.")

The average person may be shocked to learn just how widespread the problem is among those not of my gender. There must be at least several dozen cases on record, maybe even a billion, give or take a few hundred thousand. The whole thing goes all the way back to Genesis 1:27: ". . . male and female he created them."

You're telling me.

But this fine, sunny June morning, when the only thing disturbing the peace was the distant howling of a discontented canine, I wasn't about to crank up the tension.

"OK," I said, forcing a smile. "Forty-five dollars coming up!" I punched in the appropriate numbers and from somewhere deep inside the machine's innards came the sound of rising currency. Its metallic mandibles opened, and I removed and pocketed the stuff of which memorable garage sale expeditions are made.

Ten minutes later, we cruised smoothly along Colonial Court, eyes peeled for the street number listed in the classified ads section of the newspaper.

"There it is." Diana pointed off to our right. Actually, the locations of such events are not that hard to spot, though not because of the open garage door from which there spills a lava-like flow of junk. It's the wicked and satisfied grins on the part of purchasers' faces that signals you have just entered the buy-right zone. There can be little doubt that a Stradivarius-quality salad shooter or limited-edition Englebert Humperdinck eight-track tape has just been purchased for next-to-nothing, which, of course, is exactly what these objects are worth. This is why the seller's joy appears to exceed even that of their customer's.

Even before I'd brought the car to a stop, my heart performed a cardiovascular loop-de-loop. Sitting there, off to one side of the home's driveway, was exactly what I needed in order to take a giant step forward in my homesteading pursuits: a premium-quality, pre-owned, prehistoric . . . roto-tiller! I'd just found the missing link between my jungle of weeds and a family garden plot flowing with cornsilk and honeydews!

With Diana preoccupied rifling through a stack of kids' clothing, I sauntered over and began circling the piece of garden equipment. This move was designed to fake out the owner, causing him to think that I actually knew what to look for in a used tiller.

My analysis soon completed, I strolled over to the woman seated behind the card table serving as cash counter. "Can you tell me something about the tiller?" I casually asked.

The expression registered by the woman was that of an obviously seasoned garage salesperson. Hardly was there a hint that earlier that morning she and her husband had agreed to celebrate at Ernie's Fine Eatery that evening if they could peddle the garden hunk of junk by sundown.

Suddenly, the woman cried out, "Oh, honey!"

This seemed a bit forward, since I hadn't actually said I'd buy the thing.

A muscular-looking gentleman stepped around the side of the garage.

"Hon," the woman said to her husband, "this man would like to know something about the *tiller!*"

The guy's face brightened as if someone had just plugged him into a 240-volt outlet. "Sure enough, bud!" he said, and motioned me toward the machine. "Come on over here and I'll start 'er up. Runs real good," he added as we trooped along.

Having stated his objective opinion, the owner placed his foot on the tines and grabbed hold of the starter cord. With not much more effort than it takes to yank a 99-year-old saguaro cactus from the desert floor barehanded, the tiller sputtered to life. Next he opened the throttle, then demonstrated the gearshift. "She's got a lot of life left in 'er!" he called out above the engine's roar. Hitting the kill switch, the owner turned and asked, "So, whad'ya think, bud?"

"Bud" was thinking that any configuration of tines, tires and Briggs and Stratton engine was a quantum leap toward achieving his gardening goals. Still, I had yet to pop the price-tag question.

"So, uh, how much do you want for it?" I asked, feigning a lack of enthusiasm.

The gentleman's response momentarily took my breath away.

"Forty-five bucks—you haul."

I'd never thought of Diana as a prophetess, but as my mind flashed back to our earlier stop at the automatic teller machine, the possibility seemed quite real. God works in mysterious ways, this time through a source very close to me.

My Killer Tiller

It wasn't all that easy fitting the five-horsepower Leviathan into the trunk of our car, but when Providence speaks, and the price is right, you do what you gotta do. The kids could wait another week for new used clothes.

Back home, Diana flexed her feminine muscles and helped me dislodge the tiller from the car trunk. Since I wanted the piece of equipment to look respectable while doing its weed-destroying thing, I scrubbed off layers of dust and grease, and tightened bolt after bolt. Satisfied that I'd done everything I could to cherry out the machine, I moved the throttle into the start position, set my foot on the tines, and yanked the cord.

Repeating this procedure late into the night, I had nothing to show for it except the inflammation of my right shoulder rotator cuff. Finally I gave up and headed for bed, dragging my weary arm along through the dewy grass.

Several days later I gave in to a suggestion made by Diana. "Why don't you just loosen everything you tightened?" she'd said. "You know, put everything back the way it was when you bought it."

Come, come, my ego said crankily to my id. *After all these years of marriage does my own wife still think I'm totally inept as a mechanic?*

Glancing at the crop of weeds about to overtake our garden space, however, forced me to give in to Diana's idea.

With the bolts loosened, I pulled the cord. I am sorry to report that the nutty procedure suggested by my wife resulted in the engine functioning perfectly. This could not be said of my sense of manhood.

The time had come to take the tiller out for a trial run. A few minutes later I was gleefully commandeering the beast as it attempted to churn our Maryland garden soil, the consistency of which is much like concrete.

I could describe in detail that inaugural run, but you can experience it for yourself by following these directions:

Drive to your closest army surplus outlet and purchase a vintage World War II submachine gun, along with a few belts of ammo. Back home, load the ammo, then ram the weapon barrel-first deep into the ground. Holding on tightly with both hands, depress the trigger for between 60 and 120 seconds, or until you feel that your body has been grotesquely rearranged. The various sensations you experience during this time will be just about the same as if you were using a front-tine tiller in soil like ours.

No, that tiller was hardly the Mercedes-Benz of dirt-busters. But when you can afford nothing better, it's better than nothing, which is what I concluded as I shook, rattled, and rolled along.

None of this would have happened, of course, had I refused to give Diana's idea a chance. My ego almost kept our $45 miracle machine from digging in, all of which reminds me of this proverb: "Pride goes before destruction, a haughty spirit before a fall" (Proverbs 16:18).

Tiller or not, it's best to weed pride out of your life . . . and always listen to your wife.

Night of the Cucumber Crazies

My interest in home gardening doesn't come from some irresistible attraction to the soil. Rather, I'd learned early on that, along with beets and broccoli, a garden can produce a hearty crop of character. That's something Mom and Dad knew, too. Accordingly, they planted my brother, Dave, and I firmly in the gardening experience while we were still mere lads. I'm determined to provide my own kids with the same torture—uh, *opportunity*.

Dad, a certified public accountant by trade, was always dabbling in other fields. Cucumbers was the crop of choice the summer of my tenth birthday.

"With Flamm's Pickle Packing Company being so close," Dad explained one evening, "planting and picking cucumbers will be a good way for you boys to spend the summer. We've got the empty field, and you kids have the time."

My head began to spin. This was home gardening gone awry; an honorable adult hobby that had no business bursting onto the scenery of an idyllic childhood summer!

"And," Dad added, heading out the door to give his 1947 Ford tractor a pre-season check-up, "at the end of the season, you'll have some money in the bank to show for your hard work."

The idea of returning to school as a third grade cucumber magnate, king of the dill, as it were, appealed to me. I slipped between the bed sheets that night wondering how being rich would affect my relationships with those of average-allowance income, such as my country neighborhood pal, Lennie Decker. At least I'd be able to pay back the quarter I'd borrowed from Lennie, and maybe throw in a major league baseball team as interest.

"Hoe, hoe, hoe!" Dad's jolly midsummer rallying cry now fell on my ears like the monosyllabic rantings of a crazed taskmaster. Eight weeks into the cucumber venture, and I'd already attempted to turn in my resignation several times. This did not set well with the board of directors, who politely threatened to direct a board at my sitter if a change of attitude was not forthcoming.

But what really served to re-energize my brother, Dave, and me was seeing Mom and Dad themselves taking the field. They were doing their part to help turn an acre of Michigan farmland into a small-time but thriving family business. How they knew to motivate us boys this way without having taken a corporate workshop in leadership by example I'll never know. But it worked, and so did they.

One day Lennie came by. "Wow—there's a whole lot of cukes in your patch!" My sunken chest swelled with pride at my pal's comment as we surveyed the growing fruits of our summer labors. It'd been a while since my friend had seen the field, and his comment reaffirmed that our hard work was about to pay off big.

"Now you just have to make sure nobody steals 'em," Lennie cautioned with all the collective wisdom his 12 years of life had afforded him.

"Wh-what do you mean?" I'd not heard that black-market cukes were fetching big money that year.

"Well," Lennie continued, "you never know. Some crook might drive by here and see all these cucumbers and think, *I'll just slip over here tonight and pick this patch clean.*' Next morning you'll come out and find nothing but leaves and stems. And then you can kiss your cash crop goodbye."

Cucumber thief? I'd been so busy hoeing and complaining that I'd never stopped to think that our entire operation went unguarded between sundown and sunrise. While we staff members were asleep up at the house, dastardly Vince Levine could be cleaning us out, slick as a pickle! Just like Lennie said, the heist could be over before we woke up!

Earlier in the season, I wouldn't have been so concerned. But now, with the patch covered in verdant foliage and laced with bright, yellow blossoms, I had too much invested in the project to let it slip away without a fight.

Recruiting the Michigan National Guard to patrol the perimeters of the patch was an option, but about as likely as Mom and Dad calling the project off, suggesting we spend the rest of the summer reconnecting as a family on the French Riviera. Besides, by the time we got through to the governor, and the state legislature approved our request, the cukes would have grown to the size of submarines—an unsaleable condition.

In the midst of pondering our potential business-destroying predicament, my eyes drifted over to the lone cherry tree silhouetted high on the hill near our house. At that moment I knew the solution to our problem was ensconced within its branches.

"The tree house!" I cried. "We can sleep in the tree house tonight and watch for cucumber crooks!"

Lennie, whom I had failed to remember had no vested interest in our enterprise, nevertheless caught the spirit. Glancing up at the tree house, he smiled and slowly nodded in agreement. "That's a pretty good idea! I'll ask my folks if I can bring my sleeping bag—and my gun," he added with a wicked grin.

Of course! Lennie had recently had the good fortune to receive a Crossman BB pistol for his birthday. While its precision was considerably less than that of a heat-seeking missle, scoring a hit was less important than the feeling of security it would lend us tree-dwellers come eventide and beyond. There was another benefit attached to the weapon: its rapid-fire *popping* sound would cause the thief to believe someone had arisen to make a late-night bowl of popcorn, an act good enough to deter him from his bad deed.

"Here comes my sleeping bag," I called out to Lennie, who awaited my toss overhead. With the sun dipping low on the western horizon, we were stocking up for the stakeout. "Be careful with this," I added, heaving up my cherished copy of *The Hardy Boys Detective Handbook*. With that, I grabbed hold of a lower tree limb and swung up to catch the next branch that would carry me closer to my lofty goal.

My brother Dave had decided to join our regiment, fearful of missing out on any late-night entertainment this high experience might bring. "Mom sent these along," he announced, holding out a plastic bag stuffed full of enough chocolate chip cookies to last at least three minutes. A more committed group of night watchmen might have held them in reserve for launching at the cucumber culprit should the BBs run out. But we weren't actually under contract to nab the thief, so we tossed them down the hatch in hopes of sweet dreams.

"OK," Lennie announced, assuming command of the group, "what we need to do is each take a watch." I waited for him to hand a Timex to each of us, but he just kept talking. "We'll each stay awake for an hour while the other two guys sleep. Then the one on duty will wake the next person up, and the first guard will hit the sack. We'll keep changing places until sunrise. Got it?"

"Yeah, OK," I agreed.

"Sure," Dave nodded. A hundred thousand crickets and a smattering of tree frogs who'd overheard our plan echoed their support.

Suddenly I realized that one question of crucial importance remained unanswered. "Hey, Lennie," I asked, "what exactly do we do if we spot the pickle-lifter? I mean, it's not like I can just shout, 'Put up your cukes!' or anything."

A sly smile crossed Lennie's face. He reached underneath his pillow and pulled out the air pistol. Dave's and my eyes grew wide as our big-shot compatriot held the weapon high, stating cockily, "Does this answer your question?"

"*Ohhh* . . . gotcha," we both said, nodding.

Confidence running thick as tree sap, we negotiated the watch rotation. With Lennie on duty first, Dave and I slipped into our sleeping bags and set out on our journey toward the state of unconsciousness.

The plan went off like clockwork far into the night or, more accurately, until after I'd taken over and stared into a moonlit, motionless field of brain-dead vegetables for as long as I could stand, which was about six minutes. With Lennie and Dave slumbering blissfully nearby, the entire scene was more potent than the strongest sedative available with or without a prescription.

"Dave," I whispered, "are you awake?"

"I don't think so."

"I-I'm going inside," I said hesitantly. For just a moment, I thought I saw Lennie reaching underneath his pillow.

Dave propped himself up on one elbow. "OK," he said, "Lennie and I will cover your watch." Big brothers can be very understanding when you least expect it.

"Thanks," I smiled wearily.

"Here," he added, handing me the detective handbook. "Take this with you—we need all the room we can get up here."

Taking the book from my brother, I could only hope the thief's tactics wouldn't demand quick insight from the Hardy boys.

Next morning, after a fabulous night's sleep in familiar territory, I sped out to the cucumber patch. Quickly I lifted a vine and peeked underneath. The plant was loaded with cukes! A repeat performance in several other field locations told me our crop was safe! Racing back to the tree house, I clambered up its limbs to salute the cucumber patch vigilantes.

Inside the tree house, Lennie sat carving a notch in the handle of his air pistol. If you believe that, you're probably gullible enough to think someone would actually attempt to steal stupid cucumbers from a field in the middle of the night.

"Hey, guys," I shouted to the two semi-comatose figures on the tree house floor, "the cukes are still there!"

The forthcoming mumbling and general lack of positive response told me that the dynamic duo's physical and emotional reserves had been depleted during their harrowing ordeal. Without further comment I retreated, lest Lennie consider me fodder for early-morning target practice.

Since those night maneuvers of long ago, I've come to realize that there are indeed a few things in this life worthy of one's uncompromised devotion. Guarding a patch of wannabe pickles from rustlers isn't one of them.

I'm pleased to report that we went on to harvest a fine crop of cucumbers that year. In my mind's eye I can still see clearly Dad pulling up to the sorting machines at Flamm's Pickle Packing Company, our comparatively small harvest following faithfully along behind in Dad's little blue utility trailer. At the truck unloading dock, we wedged ourselves between two huge produce trucks loaded with similar fare. To the other drivers, this made for great comedy.

But you know something? Somehow, it's those kinds of memories that spur me on to encourage our three sons in their various pursuits. No, we didn't get wealthy off the cucumber venture. But what Mom and Dad modeled for their boys that summer—love, discipline, commitment, and a lot of hard work—are virtues that enrich me to this day. Of course, there's another kind of crop I hope my own family sees growing in my life: "But the fruit of the Spirit is love, joy, peace, patience, kindness, goodness, faithfulness, gentleness and self-control" (Galatians 5:22). Good stuff—no, God stuff—indeed.

Down to Business

"How can I make some money?"
Pitched in any key, that question is music to my entrepreneurial ears—especially if it's my kids doing the asking. Assuming they're not considering a career in counterfeiting, it means we've succeeded as parents in letting our children know that, with hard work and God's blessing, many of their creative dreams can become reality. Not that a strong work ethic is top priority with our kids. Still, they're willing to work up a few beads of sweat to provide the means necessary to free up a jawbreaker from vending machine captivity during our next trip to town.

Talk about timing! My latest plan had everything a parent could hope for in providing my kids with a sense of satisfaction *and* spending money.

A few weeks earlier, I'd noticed a growing pile of beat-up wooden industrial pallets heaped in one of the fields adjacent to my place of employment. A conversation with the guys back in maintenance confirmed my suspicion: the pallets were soon bound for that big landfill in the sky.

Man, I thought, *there's got to be a good use for all that wood!* Stomping down hard, I pushed my creativity pedal to the metal. Soon a glorious picture of the ultimate home-based business began to form. What person with a trace of environmental consciousness wouldn't gladly plunk down a few bucks for a *bluebird house* constructed from recycled industrial pallets? My zeal for the project increased as I pictured my three sons working alongside me in the garage as we readied yet another load of birdhouses for shipment.

"Andrew, go ask Mom to phone Continental Fasteners and tell them we'll need another eighteen-wheeler full of nails by Thursday. Tyler, go out to the driveway and count the boxes in the area I marked 'Chain Store Inventory.' When you get to 10,000, come and get me. Ethan, let go of my pantleg."

With free lumber and no payroll to meet, the profits would be more grandiose than my daydream!

After giving the venture a few days to germinate, it was a go-ahead.

A few evenings later Diana, before heading off to her part-time evening job at Christian Light Bookstore, dropped the boys off at my workplace at quitting time. I'd already changed into jeans and a T-shirt. The goal was to put my kids to work disassembling as many pallets as would fit uncomfortably into the trunk of our car. From there, we'd take the boards home, pull nails from them, plane them down, and watch our family bank account shoot sky high.

"Now be careful, boys," Diana cautioned, realizing that this was the stuff of which tetanus vaccine manufacturers' dreams are made. With a parting kiss and a shake of her head, my wife strolled back toward her car and drove off to work.

Meanwhile, the little wrecking crew got into full swing. *Smash! Bang! Ouch!* Except for that last one, the kids were having more fun than Japanese beetles at a rose show. I hoped my otherwise supportive office coworkers, upon spotting this circus performance from the not-too-distant parking lot, would refrain from swapping disrespectful comments.

"Whatd'ya think he's doin' out there, Wayne?"

"Hard to say, Mike. Maybe he's gonna build a new house on 'skid row'. Get it?"

"Got it! Ha, ha, ha!"

Yeah, yeah, yeah. Even had this kind of wry commentary drifted in my direction, I wouldn't have paid any attention. My focus was fixed on the task at hand, except when I got a splinter. Then my focus *was* my hand, and the task was removing it, or the splinter, whichever relieved the pain quickest.

"Well, boys, I think that's about it," I finally announced as the sun began disappearing behind nearby Fairview Mountain. I opened the car's back door and tossed my six-pound sledge hammer onto the floor.

"Aw, we want to do more!" the boys chorused. I appreciated their willingness to continue destroying the handiwork of a bevy of master pallet-crafters, but the trunk was full, and beyond.

"Come on," I repeated. "It's time to hop in the car." Truly we had taken to heart the wise man's counsel: "Whatever your hand finds to do, do it with all your might" (Ecclesiastes 9:10). I hoped their commitment to this counsel would continue come time to slap the tweety bird boxes together.

Pulling the trunk lid down as far down as possible, I hooked a bungee cord into the first hole I could find. With that we headed for home, our ungangly load of lumber giving the appearance that we'd crashed through a frontier stockade fort and kept on going.

"Dad, I need some help," Andrew moaned a few days later, standing near a stack of boards from which he'd been attempting to remove any remaining nails. This particular piece held an uncooperative 16-penny job.

"Here, bud," I offered, "let me show you how to use another piece of wood to help get that nail out." My performance was so impressive that I was encouraged to repeat it many times over, mostly with my work crew amusing themselves nearby. Good thing no one from the N. C. K. K. S. P. T-C. D. (National Council for Keeping Kids Safe from Power Tool-Crazed Dads) was anywhere around. They would've been less-than-impressed to see my youngsters dashing about playing tag between a running table saw and a 10-inch planer. As for Ethan, his main role had been scattering one-inch galvanized brads on the smooth garage floor, providing a challenging battery of dexterity tests for Dad's worn-out fingers.

A few hours later I walked in from the garage. In my hands I held the first prototype of our stylish bluebird abodes. The job had taken longer than I'd hoped, but that would change when we geared up for mass production. The good news was that the finished product quite resembled the store-bought one from which I'd pirated the design.

"Hey, that looks pretty good, Dad!" Tyler affirmed. This was quickly followed by "How much did you say us kids get for each one we helped build and sell?" At least they were still with the project in some limited fashion, be it purely capitalistic.

The next weekend I showed the birdhouse to my friend, Ted, who is not only a physician but also a fine woodcrafter. "Hey, that's a good-looking bluebird house," he politely diagnosed. Then he added, "You know, there are earthy-type catalogs that carry this type of thing. They'd really go for birdhouses built from recycled lumber. You ought to see if they'd be interested in adding your product to their line."

Wow! I thought. *Maybe he's on to something! Think of the volume!* But as I thought about Ted's idea, my mind drifted to a former entrepreneurial adventure...

I just can't seem to get the greenhouse bug out of my system," I sighed to Diana. We'd been married only a few months, and I'd been supplying tropical plants to a few local retailers from a couple of greenhouses I'd constructed from polyethylene plastic and electrical conduit. But it was tough competing in Michigan with foliage suppliers whose stock grew like weeds in the lush acreage surrounding Apopka, Florida. Add to that the limited shelf life of green things crammed onto supermarket display racks and, well, it just seemed like something had to change. If it didn't, I'd likely have to change something more significant—my identity, as protection against savage creditors.

What I needed was a product that would keep my hands in the soil but stay looking good for months at a time. What I needed was... *cacti!*

Some cerebral key had suddenly unlocked my safety deposit box of ideas. Cacti could go for weeks—maybe months—without care. I'd even heard one wholesale buyer say that his customers couldn't tell if the cacti they bought were dead or alive! I wasn't interested in peddling lifeless life forms, but it was clear that the novelty of owning displaced desert matter was uppermost in some buyers' minds. The only thing that could make the whole concept better was if I could include my love of woodworking in the scheme. As if on cue, this piece of the product puzzle also fell into place. *I'll arrange three pots of cacti in a little wooden* holder, I mentally proposed. *Every housewife in America will want one sitting on her kitchen windowsill!*

Realizing I might just be on to the biggest gimmick, er, product advance since the pet rock, I called my C.P.A. for advice.

"Dad, could I come over and talk to you about something?" Not only was the service good, but the price was right.

That evening, my father, who is also prone to stepping out on occasion in pursuit of a new venture, added my proposal's facts and figures together. His pronouncement was just what I'd hoped to hear. "If you limit your costs to what you've listed, son, you can make this thing work."

My costs, of course, were made with the assumption in mind that my employee roster would be limited to somewhere around one. But that was OK—I could divide my time between being CEO and garage floor sweeper just fine.

Soon my product design was complete. I arranged to have some small cacti air-freighted to our home, where I put the whole concept together. Within a few weeks "Desert Sun" cacti planters were selling like hotcakes in several local outlets.

Boy, I thought, *if these things sell this well around here, maybe I ought to try getting them into a chain of stores!*

With no real marketing background to persuade me otherwise, I boldly phoned up the corporate headquarters of a major retail chain. "Could I make an appointment to see someone about buying some of my cacti planters?" Apparently the receptionist on the other end of the line had no real marketing background to persuade her otherwise, for upon hanging up I had an appointment to plead and present my case of cacti before a real, live wholesale buyer.

I called my C.P.A. "Dad, do you think you could come along with me?" I asked hopefully. My father possesses singular business savvy. He is also bald. While a big-time buyer might turn up his corporate nose at me, he'd likely possess the common courtesy to not arbitrarily pass off someone as mature-looking and wise as Dad. All told, the father-son, one-two punch seemed like a good business strategy.

The day of the appointment arrived, and Dad and I wheeled into the multi-story corporate building's parking lot. I hauled my box of picture-perfect cacti planters out of the trunk, and with a quick glance over at Dad for reassurance, we strolled up to the impressive-looking structure's front doors.

Inside, we were directed to Mr. Bookman's office.

"Welcome, Mr. Fishell," the man greeted me. He then reached over to shake hands with my father. "And you must be—"

"Mr. Fishell," he responded politely.

"Oh, I see." Mr. Bookman cleared his throat. "Well, have a seat." After a bit of small talk, the buyer finally popped the question that counted. "So, what exactly do you have that you think our chain of stores should carry?"

My already damp armpits suddenly became vast reservoirs of perspiration. This was it—my destiny as a mega-pusher of prickly pear hung in the balance.

I slowly opened the box of cacti planters and pulled back the container's flaps, fully revealing the fruit of my labors. Dad's gaze remained firmly on Mr. Bookman.

The buyer gently lifted a planter from its resting place and studied it in silence. Slowly but surely, a smile crossed the buyer's face.

"I like it!" he declared.

The breath I'd been holding burst through my lips in quiet celebration.

"So," the man continued, "what do you think you need for 'em?"

With that, the negotiations began. Of course, I'd arrived with the idea in mind that I'd sell the planters for whatever he could afford to pay, and that's pretty much how the negotiations ended. The only disappointment was that Mr. Bookman wouldn't actually commit to an order. Frustrated, I finally made an amateur attempt to close the deal. "So, Mr. Bookman," I said with all the rookie confidence I could muster, "where do we go from here?"

The man looked back at me as if to say, "Well, I don't know where you're going, but I'm going fishing! Ha, ha!"

"I'm going fishing!" Mr. Bookman stated with glee. "Tomorrow is the first day of my vacation!" Refocusing on the matter at hand, he said, "I'll need to show these to a couple of the other buyers. We'll let you know what we decide." With that, he showed us to the door, which I perceived to be a strong suggestion that we walk through it and out of the building.

The next day, Dad's secretary called me at home. I'd been using my father's office number to ensure someone would always be at the ready to take cacti planter orders.

"Randy," Clara, Dad's secretary said, "a Mr. Bookman just called."

My heart began to palpitate.

"Oh, really?" I replied, feigning control of my emotions.

"Yes, and he placed an order for some of those cacti planters you've been making."

"I see. Uh, how many?"

"Well, he'd like to have, let's see now, how many was it? Oh, yes—174 . . . *cases*. And he said he'd like to have them very soon."

Upon recovering from my severe shock, I politely thanked Clara and hung up. I can't exactly remember what I called my victory dance—"Cactus Cash Crop Hop" or something like that.

Before I called Diana at work to tell her the good news, I grabbed my calculator and punched in the numbers. *How many cacti planters are actually in 174 cases?* I wondered. *Let's see . . . twelve in a case times 174 . . .* Could this be possible? Would my tiny garage-based company soon be involved in producing over *2,000* cacti planters? Another couple of calculations revealed that the project would require 6,000 cacti, 25,000 pieces of precision-cut planter parts, and 37,000 nails!

I pondered the full range of consequences that my marketing fortitude had reaped. Maybe I should've tried something else, a venture where I could at least catch a few Z's between sunset and daybreak. It certainly didn't look as if that were going to happen for a long time.

Quickly I phoned my C.P.A. "Dad, uh, do you think you could spare a little time this month, say four weeks?" I went on to explain that his assistance would serve a broader purpose than just helping to get the order out on time. It would also spare him the embarrassment of having to explain why his adult son was running down the street like a crazed lunatic while making threatening remarks and wielding a pointed cactus in each hand.

Not only did Dad show up, but Mom came along as well, her cacti-planting uniform made complete by the well-padded gloves covering her willing hands.

But even this proved to be not quite enough. The evening before the scheduled delivery date found the garage chocked full of temporary employees determined to help get the order out on time. Wood buzzing through the table saw, two pre-owned pneumatic nailers whipping planters together, and the *slosh-slosh* of their being dipped in buckets of stain were evidence of a fully-committed crew.

And they got the job done. The following week, advertisements touting my little entrepreneurial dream-come-true appeared in newspaper ads all across Michigan. It was the chain store's official "Plant of the Week" special.

Yet all was not bliss in succulentland. The cacti business was moving in fits and starts. The big stores had a fit when I tried to coax them into paying before their standard 90 days, and I started to panic. Add to that the free replacement of an entire order damaged in shipment, and other occasional financial crises, and life in the big store leagues wasn't all I had cracked it up to be.

Could it be, I wondered one evening, *that selling cacti isn't my life's calling?* I decided to take my future to the Lord as never before, asking Him to point me in the right direction.

Now, I've never been one to encourage folks to expect on-the-spot answers to every prayer. But what I'm about to share with you is the gospel, no-fingers-crossed truth.

While on my knees, having just included in my evening prayers my desire to follow heaven's leading, the phone rang. It was God, speaking through one of his "earthen vessels."

"Randy, this is Pastor Geoff calling."

"Oh, uh, yeah. How's everything going with you there? Haven't talked to you since . . . yesterday." The previous evening I'd phoned my former youth leader and mentor, now a youth pastor in the Riverside, California, area to learn more about professional youth ministry. I'd been serving as a youth worker in my local church, and had discovered that it brought great fulfillment. It would be a huge leap from selling cacti to spreading the gospel. But I figured it couldn't hurt to get the scoop on ministry as a vocation.

"Randy," Geoff said, "I'm calling about our conversation yesterday. You were asking about youth work, and after we hung up I had an idea. Would you and Diana like to come and spend the summer working in youth ministry with me?"

Just as so many little cacti had been removed from their seedling beds and shipped cross-country to my garage, I sensed just then that God was uprooting me for service elsewhere in His vineyard. There would be college and seminary, but one day I would accept a Seattle church's invitation to serve as its youth pastor. It wasn't the last stop in my vocational journey, but it was part of God's plan.

So it turned out cacti *wasn't* my ultimate calling. But I'd sure had a ton of fun moving my potted concept from idea to reality. That had to mean *something*, didn't it?

Back in the present, I took the bluebird house back from Ted and tossed it in the trunk of my car. "Well, I guess I'd better be heading home," I told him, slamming the trunk lid shut. "I'll keep in mind what you said about getting the birdhouses into a catalog." With a friendly wave goodbye, I pulled out of the good doctor's driveway.

As I cruised toward home, I thought about cacti and bluebird houses and lots of other projects in which I'd dabbled. Some of them had actually become profitable; others had earned me mostly the sense of satisfaction that comes with seeing an idea take form and shape.

Yes, it *did* mean something that I'd so enjoyed my various endeavors, regardless of the financial outcome. I was breathing life, as it were, into an idea. Be it a garage or basement or barn (I've used 'em all), such a place is a crucible for creating, an activity that reflects something of God's own personhood.

"In the beginning God created . . . God saw all that he had made, and it was very good" (Genesis 1:1, 31).

God's creative acts, of course, brought something out of nothing—*ex nihilo*, to use a theological term. My creative endeavors aren't quite *that* original! Still, I can't help but think that the joy I feel as I complete and in turn share with the world my simple creations, is a heavenly gift. I want my kids to experience that joy, and come to sense its value. There's more than one way to profit from a creative pursuit.

The other day Don, who works in the computer division at my workplace, leaned into my open office door. "Hey, Randy, you got any of those bluebird houses left? You know, like the ones you were selling around here a few weeks ago?"

After the boys and I had built some bluebird houses, I'd placed a few of them in strategic locations around my workplace, offering them for sale. My goal was to use the proceeds to help a needy family—mine. This condition resulted in part from the fact that the birdhouses, which I sold for under $10, ended up costing somewhere around a month's salary each to make. I guess there was a reason those pallets were in the burn pile—whipping them into a condition suitable for bluebird houses seemed to take more discretionary time than I had left in my earthly pilgrimage.

But then again, if I *did* take Don's order, I'd be making something from *almost* nothing.

"Uh, yeah, sure Don," I replied thoughtfully. "I'll give you a call when I've got some ready."

Which could be pretty soon. Now, where are those boys of mine? We've got a home-based business to run here. First, though, I think I'll call my C.P.A. He's a good man to have around, especially if this bluebird house thing busts loose.

The Days of Whine and Road Dust

"All systems go?" The commander's voice is shaky. The dire circumstances surrounding this mission are already taking their toll.

"Yeah, I guess we're ready." The tentative response coming from the beautiful second-in-command seated nearby merely reaffirms the crew's spirit of resignation.

The commander sighs, then speaks the fateful order. "OK, let's do it." His strong, though slightly trembling hand reaches toward the ignition switch. The perilous journey is about to begin. There will be no turning back.

It is because of this reality that from somewhere a small voice calls out, "I forgot to go to the bathroom!"

The crew members' shoulders slump. The Fishell's family vacation will be delayed another five minutes.

Although I can't prove it, I think the term "family vacation" comes from the Latin term *vacatocranio troopus*, meaning "to depart from rational thinking as a unit." Why else would two adults and three children under the age of 10 fuse themselves together for hours at a time in a rolling sheet metal cubicle and call it fun? (Repeating the procedure on day two involves *"re-*fusing," a term anyone thinking about a family vacation should consider employing before strapping on the cartop carrier.)

Our tribe's vacations are of the budget variety. This means virtually stress-free decision-making. Questions such as "Shall we try the Waikiki Hilton this year, hon?" or "Kids, do you want to take the ATV or the mini-sub along on the trip; we have room behind the motor home for only one of them" never need to be resolved by tightwad vacationers. The biggest concern for us budgeteers is whether the day's travel feasting will consist of processed cheese or peanut-butter-and-jelly sandwiches.

Family vacations furnish exceptional ministry opportunities. Each year I give my parents the chance to open their home to us, holding out their grandkids as bait. I'm not sure if they've ever said yes, but they never actually said no. So off we head to a quaint, remodeled farmhouse in southwestern Michigan, where we receive great love and the amenities of a Cape Cod resort for not even a nickel a night.

The saying "Getting there is half the fun" is a gross exaggeration of the facts. It's not easy to bump down the toll road in a stuffed-full, decade-old car with a playpen strapped to the trunk and retain any sense of dignity. "Leaving it all behind" hardly applies, since we've taken most of it with us. Shiny mini-vans pass us on the left, little kids pointing from plush rear bench seats, saying things like, "Look, Mom and Dad! Isn't that those funny people from the show we watched on Nickelodeon yesterday?"

"No, the *Beverly Hillbillies* are just TV characters," their mother replies. "I *think*," she adds, spotting our car in her side view mirror.

Nevertheless, even at the risk of losing our self-esteem, Diana and I think it's good to follow the advice of Jesus to his weary disciples: "And he said unto them, Come ye yourselves apart . . . and rest a while" (Mark 6:31, KJV).

We figure if we don't 'come apart' we might soon *fall* apart.

On the one hand, as I initially implied, there are lots of reasons why vacationing with the kids should be postponed until the time they're taking their graduate school exams. But children have a weird way of making the kind of memories you can't afford to miss out on, so it's best just to have a plan of action.

We've learned there are specific things that can be done to help make the trip seem to go faster. One of these is to take an airplane. Since saving up for plane fare for our family of five would take somewhere around a geological age, flying the friendly skies is out. Accordingly, creative games, aimed at distracting the kids and preserving their parents' sanity are next on the list.

Most travel games that I've developed capture our kids' interest for at least a minute and a half. This means that providing entertainment throughout the nearly 600 miles to the grandparents' place calls for at least 450 games and activities.

The activity we encourage most is called "Who Can Sleep the Most Between Maryland and Michigan?" Still, our three boys don't play it as much as we'd like.

"License Plate List" is a game that has met with some success. The object of this game is to see how many states' license plates you can spot. In the end, it proves to be a complete waste of time, which is precisely what you hope to accomplish.

"What's that plate?" Tyler asked during a recent vacation. He craned his neck as a Toyota Camry whizzed by.

Squinting my eyes, I reported, "Ohio." Number one son quickly jotted the name on the list.

"How 'bout that one?" Andrew piped up from somewhere beneath a pile of books and a collection of petrified Kleenexes.

Diana spoke up. "Looks like . . . Ohio." As it turned out, Buckeye state plates proved to be in great abundance as we traversed the interminable distance between Youngstown and Toledo.

"Look at *that* one!" Tyler yelled. "What is it?" My eyes grew wide with disbelief. After oodles of Ohio and Indiana plates, we'd spotted the "big one"—H*awaii!* Emotions ran wild, and tears came to my eyes, mostly because I had just realized that our travels had caused us to become irrational over a piece of penitentiary-produced metalwork.

A few miles later, looking ahead, I noticed we'd caught up to the car bearing the trophy license plate. *Wait a minute,* I thought, looking more closely this time. *Something looks funny about that plate.* "Funny" is used advisedly here, since the discovery of a Pennsylvania tag hiding beneath a Hawaii license plate frame is less than amusing within a circle of five roving lunatics.

Our summertime arrival at my folks' place in Michigan is only half the story. My childhood home lies midway between our present home in Maryland and our more-often-than-not ultimate vacation goal: Minnesota.

North woods cabin fervor runs high in Diana's extended family, a condition which can be traced to my wife's grandparents owning a cabin overlooking scenic and remote Deer Lake. Although Grandpa and Grandma Blost have passed on, this treasured piece of upstate real estate remains in the family, hence our frequent pilgrimages to the Land of 10,000 Lakes.

Our yearly trek is a constant reminder of the astonishing power of family tradition. Somehow, this indefinable but very real force causes Diana's clan to overlook the zillion Hindenburg-size mosquitoes and lack of indoor plumbing, and heed the call of the loon.

A few years back, Diana and her two sisters, Holly and Heather, began laying plans for a summer sibling reunion and general extended family gathering at the cabin. (To get to the cabin by car, take Minnesota highway 65 north for about two years, or until you come to the Togo Junction Bar and Grill. Turn left, and keep going for as long as it takes you to repeat the book of Deuteronomy from memory. About then you'll see Deer Lake Charlie's Flea Market. Turn right and begin looking for a disheveled-looking man attempting to play Whiffle ball in the middle of the narrow dirt road. A random assortment of children and an occasional brother-in-law or other relative joining in the action for lack of anything better to do confirms that you have reached your destination. Ignore the witty though uncomplimentary remarks about the many legions of deerflies attempting to nest in the players' hair. This is all part of the northern Minnesota vacation aura, so accept it for what it is.)

Back at the planning table, the sound of "Cool! Yippeee! Squeak-squeak!" bounced around the room. My three sons had cast their vote for Diana and her sisters' proposed summer experience. As for me, I tried to shake off the memory of a previous Deer Lake drama . . .

Diana, her brother, Ted, and I has arisen early and hit the lake for a morning fishing expedition. Ted had just hauled in a "keeper," a northern pike. Unfortunately, the poor fish had chosen to gulp down the spoon and hook along with the tasty bait. The process required to remedy this situation can best be described as repugnant. I could describe it at its worst, but you may not have made a final decision to give up seafood, and this would do it, believe me.

"Just grab that guy for a second, Randy," Ted instructed. "I'll use the pliers." Looking around, I realized the only other "guy" within the sound of my voice lay flopping around on the bottom of our aluminum fishing vessel. Reaching down, I drew within an inch of the wild-eyed victim. That's when I discovered its wimpy-looking mouth contained a fully-functional set of razor-like teeth, which were currently embedded in my hand.

"*Yeoowwww!*" came a milk-curdling cry from somewhere in the middle of Deer Lake. (It was time for the others back at the cabin to get up anyway). Flipping the creature off my hand, I surveyed the wound. It had drawn blood!

I can tell you right now that a brother-in-law convulsed in laughter on a pile of boat seat cushions and fishing gear is practically useless for rendering emergency first-aid. Thankfully, Diana's steady composure allowed her to care for my wound, the most severe of which, as it turned out, was to my ego.

But that was then, and I'd grown in my understanding of just how important the cabin is to Diana. On our wedding day I'd signed up to be part of the family. It was time to embrace the cabin experience as my own. Batten down the playpen—Deer Lake here we come!

W*hoo-o-o-o-o . . . whoo-o-o-o-o-o.* The sound of distant loons wafted across Deer Lake toward the cabin's screened-in rear porch-turned-extra bedroom.

"That sound should help you get to sleep," I told Tyler and Andrew, pulling the covers up around their chins. Our July getaway had come, and now our ears tuned in to the sound of waves lapping along the lakeshore and majestic pines gently swaying in the evening breeze.

Diana lay aside Ethan in one of the bedrooms inside; her mom had crashed in the other one. Still other extended family members, along with Raoul, a special friend of sister-in-law Heather, sat around sharing conversation and baby-sitting in another nearby cabin rented for the occasion.

Leaning over to kiss my two oldest boys goodnight, I whispered into Tyler's ear. "You know something?"

"What?"

"This place stinks."

Tyler's eyes grew wide in the darkness. "You'd better not let Mom hear you say that," he warned.

"No, that's not what I mean. There's a really bad odor out here. Don't you smell it?" I began sniffing around the open-beamed room, trying to pinpoint the stench's source. Hopping up on the bed, my nostrils were drawn toward an assortment of tools and boat repair paraphernalia perched on one of the wall's top ledges.

"Ah ha!" Still balancing on the bed, I leaned far over and took a whiff from a small container of outboard motor oil. "I think I've found the problem, boys," I announced. "But if the smell isn't really bothering you, we'll just leave this oil up here out of little hands' reach."

"OK, Dad. Good-night."

I climbed off the bed. "Good-night, boys," I said, giving their little hands a loving squeeze.

But the next morning, as I swung open the old wooden porch door, the stink hit my schnoz full-force. I lost confidence in my theory of the previous evening. *This smell is too strong to be outboard motor oil*, I reasoned. I began sleuthing around the room. If the case of the offensive odor were to be solved, I needed clues.

By now Tyler and Andrew had jumped out of bed, eager for a day of wading and assorted mischief. While they dressed for the occasion, I slipped outside, hoping to spot some bit of evidence.

What I discovered is hardly the stuff of which fine perfume is made. On the ground, directly beneath an 18-inch wide section of pine siding separating the porch's two rear windows, lay a small pile of brown debris. It's aromatic essence signaled that it had at one time existed in far different form. Suddenly I realized that what I'd discovered was nothing less than a drop shipment from an undercover guano factory! All signs pointed to the fact that behind the back porch siding there existed a full-fledged bat habitat!

Where was my no-fear naturalist brother-in-law when I needed him? Six hundred miles distant, to be exact, pushing nuts and bolts at the short-staffed hardware store from which he drew a paycheck. (How Ted, who stands 6'2" in height, secured a position at a store staffed by short clerks remains a mystery.)

As the senior male on the vacation site, I knew upon whom the task of evicting the bats fell: me. Mustering my courage, I raised my chin and strode purposefully into the cabin for a second opinion.

Ten minutes later, a small crowd of onlookers, rather, a crowd of small onlookers, stood gazing at Diana as she pressed her ear to the inside porch wall. Had the stuffed great blue heron and its taxidermied comrades peering down from high in the cabin's rafters been in a happier state of existence, the alarm would've sounded.

"Don!" Skeeter the gray squirrel whispers to his rafter mate, a glassy-eyed mallard. "Those loony—sorry, Larry—humans are on to the bats' hangout! Pass the word!"

Diana, still taking soundings for bat activity, slowly nodded. "Yes, I hear bats," she announced. "Listen." She pulled me toward the wall.

Within a few minutes, listening to the cabin's back porch wall became the biggest drawing card in camp since last Wednesday's flea market at Deer Lake Charlie's. As for me, one question loomed large: What would be the environmentally-correct method for displacing these novel but hygienically-unconcerned mammals?

This being Tuesday, I decided to put off the task until the day of our departure: Friday. I figured it would take me at least that long to put together a coalition of family members and friends to assist in the campaign. The other reason for the delay was that coming face to face with a colony of bats appealed to me about as much as crossing a dirt road in the middle of a mosquito-infested Minnesota night to visit Old John the outhouse.

By the time Friday rolled around, I had formulated a breakthrough plan of attack: I'd rip the detestable section of cabin siding off, then run as if Bat Masterson was about to take me down for a bounty.

Mention at breakfast of the morning's planned event stirred activity in all corners of camp.

"Hang on, there, hey?" Michael, Holly's husband, urged. He tossed a final forkful of scrambled eggs down the hatch. "Just let me run and get my video camera."

Not my idea of sharing in the victory, but "America's Funniest Home Videos" pays better than I do.

By the time I'd loosened the boards enough to where they'd drop to the ground with a couple of well-placed hammer whacks, I realized the gravity of my situation. Gazing around, I noticed my eager audience had armed themselves with sticks and other blunt objects. The intent, of course, was to wield these weapons in self-defense should any disgruntled bats come within striking distance. It occurred to me, however, that *I* would be a convenient target should the show fall short of the mob's expectations. Within the hour I'd either be considered the Ed Sullivan of the north woods or I'd have just hosted the mother of all bores. I hoped Deer Lake Charlie had a supply of new or used band-aids in stock.

"OK, everybody," I announced, "here she goes!"

"Is the red light on?" Michael asked.

Holly leaned over to check her husband's camcorder. "Everything looks okay*yyyyyyyyaaaaaaaiiiiiiiieeeeee!*

A later viewing of the videotape showed that, although the red light was indeed on, actual images of the first wave of departing bats were about as frequent as New Year's Day. It's hard to be concerned with artistic quality and play dodge the bat at the same time.

One-by-one the disoriented, bug-eyed little beasts appeared from behind a now-exposed vertical log beam and took to the unfamiliar daytime skies.

Reaction from the crowd wavered between feverish excitement and sheer panic. Cries of "Incoming at two o'clock!" and the more common "Look out, here comes another one!" were regularly followed by frantic screams—some of delight, others of sheer terror, depending on who was blowing air.

I must say that from my vantage point, which was off to the side of the opening, the entire scenario made for better viewing than a classic collection of Three Stooges routines. This perspective changed when Heather pointed to my foot and shouted, "Randy! On your shoe!"

There, struggling to make sense of this entire fiasco, was one of the many baby bats that had dropped to the ground during the flush-out. The adrenaline rush accompanying the sighting of a bat seeking refuge in one's pantleg is considerably higher than that of any other situation I can think of.

"Randy—on your pocket!"

Although spotting a bat attempting to secure squattter's rights in your front pants pocket ranks right on up there too. I would take this opportunity to rebuke my relatives for their unempathetic attitude, but the fact that several of them still walk around doubled-up from their incessant laughter is punishment enough.

After poking a stick behind the beam and coaxing the last reticent victim from its home, the cabin was officially declared a "bat-free zone." The count ended up somewhere around 35 bats, including offspring. Where many of the creatures took up new residence is hard to say, though if they had any sense they headed for the nearby boathouse and began laying plans to turn it into a *bat*house.

As I replaced the porch siding, I experienced a great sense of loss, and not a moment too soon. Nothing personal, bats—you do have your place. Just not *this* place.

"Holly called me today, Diana," her mom said over the phone. "They watched the cabin video and laughed and laughed!" Then she added, "They're going to send us a copy so we can enjoy it too!"

Almost autumn now, our summer retreat to Minnesota was merely a memory, yet a very good one. When the tape arrived, we laughed too. We could've gone down to Video Master and rented a comedy, but the story line couldn't hold a candle to the brilliant work we'd crafted as an extended family. Unlike a scripted Hollywood version, our vacation was *real*. Real strange, to be sure, but nevertheless authentic in all aspects. And in a world given to the contrived, celebrating reality can be worth the drive.

But another, more basic purpose of vacations involves a too-often neglected pursuit in our society: embracing rest. God did His best from the beginning to ensure that humankind would take some time off. After a busy week of creating, God Himself "rested from all the work of creating that he had done" (Genesis 2:3). He asks us to follow His example, not merely two weeks each year, but weekly, on His Sabbath.

As we've learned year after year, genuine rest sometimes doesn't come easily on vacation. That may be one reason God commands us to take an every-seven-days break. And according to Scripture, a similar experiences occurs as we choose to rest in Jesus.

"There remains, then, a Sabbath-rest for the people of God: for anyone who enters God's rest also rests from his own work, just as God did from his. Let us, therefore, make every effort to enter that rest . . ." (Hebrews 4:9-11).

Each well-kept Sabbath in our home does more than rejuvenate us for another week of busy activity. It serves to remind us that we're called to take a vacation from our own good works as a way to earn heavenly favor, and instead celebrate Christ's gracious activity in our lives. The good news is, we don't even have to pack a suitcase to honor the Sabbath. If we want to feel like we're on vacation, we just check out the license plates on the way to church.

Lost and Found

Our new tenant was likeable enough, but hardly free of eccentricities. One of his more irritating mannerisms was hauling a dead mouse around between his front teeth. Still, given his roots, or lack thereof, I suppose it was only natural.

The cultureless cat first appeared at our front door in the arms of an unkempt child. The waif's pathetic sales pitch wrenched the resistance right out of both Diana and me. "I found this kitten and I've asked a lot of people, but nobody wants him." She paused, then followed with a no-frills invitation aimed at closing the deal on-the-spot. "Do *you* want him?"

We looked at the little gray-and-white fuzzball ensconced within the little girl's arms, then at each other. Did we have a bona fide excuse for not taking in this pitiful-looking feline? Having children of our own was a concept whose time had not yet come. No way could we honestly appeal to overcrowded living conditions as a reason for turning the stray away. Our house was tiny, but it's not like the kitten was going to demand a room of its own. How about the fact that we already had a dog and cat eating up a portion of our meager budget? Could we afford to feed another non-contributing member of the household? The problem with this, and every other practical argument we could muster, was that until just a couple of days previous, a third pet had called our place home.

While Diana and I had been vacationing in Minnesota, Tony, a young friend and student at the nearby university, had agreed to care for the needs of Lucy, the youngest of our two cats. Tony was a responsible young Christian man, and we felt confident placing the keys to our home in his hand.

The evening of our return, with great remorse Tony explained why Lucy wasn't there to greet us upon our arrival. It seems that the previous night, Tony decided to host a gala event at our home to celebrate his success as a pet-sitter. Even though by worldly standards it was a kosher party, the whole affair proved to be too much for Lucy. At an opportune moment she dashed out the front door and into the darkness of the neighborhood Saturday night.

"I'm really sorry," Tony sincerely apologized.

"We know you did the best you could," Diana comforted, though this turn of events hardly put us in a festive mood.

The search was on. But after marching through the neighborhood calling out Lucy's name, we were still minus one family member. Now, as the little girl stood there with the kitten on our front porch, we wondered if this was divine consolation for our loss.

A brief husband-and-wife pow-wow soon rendered a verdict in favor of giving the hapless critter at least a temporary home. We figured the least we could do was take the kitten off the girl's hands and begin a more strategic search for its rightful owner. As an enrolled seminary student, it seemed doubly important that I exhaust the possibility that this animal did not in fact belong to someone else. It would be a disadvantage to enter my first pastorate with a history as a cat burglar.

But a serious sleuthing effort turned up nothing. Either the real owners weren't 'fessing up, or the kitten truly was of the homeless stripe. Not for long. Even as we created missing cat posters and plastered them around the neighborhood in behalf of our lost Lucy, the newcomer was searching out the perfect windowsill on which to blissfully purr his days away. Time would prove that Lucy and Tigger, as we named the rascal in honor of his literary counterpart, showed such similar ability in the matter of getting themselves lost that they seemed related from the start.

"Randy, telephone call for you." A couple of days had passed since Tigger arrived at our place. Now a voice called out my name from somewhere across the showroom of the furniture store where I worked part-time. Strolling past an array of dinettes and sofas, I pulled up to the store's office. "I think it's your wife," my boss stated, handing me the telephone. Normally I would've stared at the handset and quipped something such as, "Wow, she's really changed since this morning." It's hard to be humorous, though, when someone precious to you is lost.

But with Diana's voice came new hope. "Wendy Wagner just called from over on Elm Street!" she said breathlessly. "She thinks Lucy may be underneath their house! Can you come home and help me look?"

Quickly hanging up the phone, I pled my case to the woman who signed my paycheck. Fortunately, her tenderhearted side was always close to the surface of her soul, and a moment later I was speeding down U.S. 31 toward home, and hopefully a family reunion.

"Here, Lucy. Here, kitty-kitty-kitty," Diana called sweetly into the dark, unknown recesses of the Wagner's crawlspace. Rumor had it that the old, two-story wood frame house was slated for the wrecking ball sometime in the not too distant future. But a few moments previous, our hearts had doubled their pace when two green eyes had reflected back to meet our own. Apparently, at the time she had taken flight, Lucy was less concerned about architectural integrity than escaping a houseful of wild-eyed college students.

"We have a lot of stray cats around here," Mrs. Wagner explained as we continued our efforts to woo Lucy toward us. "I wouldn't have given it a second thought, 'cept I saw your poster down on the telephone pole by the corner."

"Well, it's definitely Lucy," Diana replied, smiling, but frustrated. "She's too scared to come out, though."

Sensing an heroic opportunity before me, I urged Diana to let me give it a try. Leaning my head far into the crawlspace, I tried to sell my feline customer on the benefits of coming home with us. It reminded me of the reaction of my fellow students in preaching class the previous semester, when I'd delivered my first practice sermon. Nothing was happening.

"Hon," Diana finally said, "let me put the dish of cat food down by your feet. Lucy may be hungry enough to come over toward it. We can grab her while she's eating."

Something told me this suggestion would provide many hours of spirited discussion during Christian ethics class next semester. I began framing my question: "Is it right to create the perception that the fulfillment of one's basic need, in this case the need for food, is the sole reason for the cat food being placed in such proximity? Or does, in this case, the situation allow for deception in the present for benefit to the subject, in this case, Lucy the cat, sometime in the future?"

"Here, Lucy, here, kitty, kitty, kitty. Come and get some food."

The proponents of situation ethics would like my wife.

The bait-and-switch worked like a charm. Soon Lucy was purring like a—well, you know, in my beloved's arms. We hoped the incident would quickly fade from our traumatized pet's memory. Thanking Mrs. Wagner for the concern that led her to make the call, Diana then hugged Lucy, and I hugged Diana. We headed toward home, the family circle once again complete.

Regarding our rescue method, truth be told, I was ready and willing myself to do whatever it took to bring our little lost one home. I remember hearing something a lot like that in Salvation 101 class. Of course, Jesus doesn't *trick* anyone into accepting His redemption. But read about His mission and methods in Scripture and you'll discover that He's determined to not give up any of His wandering ones without a fight.

Had there been a school for feline dysfunction anywhere within a 200-mile radius of our home, we would have quickly requested an application form for Tigger. Considering the mauling of live rodents the highest form of entertainment, even this abhorrent behavior paled in comparison to another area of the cat's twisted personality.

The very day we took him in, he showed serious signs of intense insecurity. Our first clue was the fact that anytime either of us sat or lay down, Tigger would pounce on us, knead our shirt or pajamas, and begin sucking them. Clearly the weaning process had not been completed at the time Tigger had been tossed out to make it on his own. Suffice it to say that we strove to keep him under lock-and-key every time we tried to establish meaningful friendships with other seminary couples. Keeping the little sucker off them was a lot easier than trying to explain why he was slobbering all over their attractive blouse or new preaching suit.

On occasion, however, life has a strange way of turning undiluted weirdness into something of value.

With most of my seminary classwork completed, I had made the decision not to immediately enter pastoral ministry. Because we'd been living in university-owned housing, and I wouldn't be enrolled in coursework, we needed to find another place to call home. At this time, our combined income was on a level with that of the Dead Sea, so we decided to rent an old house inconveniently located far out in the country. But it was affordable *and* they allowed pets! An added benefit was that just across the dirt road and down by the river, a small boat dock, dilapidated as it was, came with the property. For all its shortcomings, the entire setup had a certain undeniable charm.

Tigger quickly settled in. The surrounding fields and dense woods provided an endless array of victims for his recreational enjoyment and culinary satisfaction. Slowly but surely, however, Tigger began wandering father and farther away from home in search of rare game. Sooner or later he'd always drag himself back home, where he'd rest up before hitting the road to set up yet another backwoods ambush.

But one night, Tigger *didn't* come home. After a week in absentia, we decided the primo chef of disgusting delicacies was missing in action. "Let's put a lost and found ad in the *Trade Lines* shopper," Diana suggested. "Maybe someone has him and will recognize his description." I reasoned that if anyone had Tigger in his or her possession, it wouldn't be for long. But her idea seemed worth a try.

A few days later the phone rang. "I saw your ad," a woman's terse voice said. "Can you describe your cat to me?"

Diana, who had answered the mysterious-sounding woman's call, began providing as many details as possible about Tigger's physical characteristics. This included a description of his stuffed-up tear gland that would've made even the most seasoned veterinarian consider a new career.

"Oh," Diana added, "Tigger also has a, well, 'habit' of . . ." She went on to explain about our pet's preference for sucking on anything that might provide a moment of motherly comfort.

With bated breath Diana awaited the furtive caller's reply. But the only words forthcoming were, "I'll call you back later." With that, the stranger hung up. As Diana shared the upshot of their conversation, I could only wonder if Tigger had fallen into the hands of a professional catnapper, a culprit who was even now formulating the appropriate ransom amount. Meanwhile, the sunny rays striking our dining room windowsill bounced back from whence they came, for no Tigger lay there to absorb them.

A short time later, the phone rang again. Diana quickly recognized the voice as belonging to the same woman caller. Even over the phone, it was clear that this was no easy call for the woman to make. "I-I think we may have your cat," she said softly. And then she began unfolding the story for my wife.

"We didn't mean to take your cat," she explained, "but we really thought he was ours. You see, the kids and I were out gathering leaves beside the road near your home, and we saw a cat. About a year ago, our children had another kitten. He was the same color as this one, and his tear duct was closed." She sniffed, then continued. "Well, my husband got fed up with the cat, and one day just up and took him away. He told us later that he'd taken the cat out by the river and turned him loose. By his description, I'm sure it was near your home."

Diana began to understand, fighting tears herself.

The caller continued. "When we spotted your cat by the road, we were just sure it was God's way of bringing our pet back to us." She paused. "But yesterday a friend at work who knew about our finding the cat told me about your ad. I guess this whole thing wasn't God's answer after all. I-I'm sorry this happened."

"It's OK," Diana softly replied.

Suddenly the woman's voice stiffened. "Meet me at Perry's gas station at two o'clock."

"Alright," Diana agreed. With that, the caller hung up.

At two o'clock sharp we pulled up to the north side of the small brick gas station. Rolling to a stop, we noticed a woman sitting in a car with two small children shifting nervously in the back seat.

Shutting off the engine, Diana and I got out of our car and strolled toward the woman. She opened her car door and stepped out. After a curt greeting, the woman pointed toward the back seat of her car. "Do you think that's your cat?" she asked, her voice still defensive.

Assuming she was not referring to either of her children, Diana and I peered more closely into the woman's car. There, seated comfortably between the two kids, was Tigger!

"That's him!" Diana blurted out with joy. "You've found our cat!"

The woman, still apparently unwilling to concede that the cat in her car was not her own, reached in and retrieved Tigger. "Are you *absolutely* sure?" she asked.

Without hesitation, Diana affirmed her conviction that this was indeed our lost pet.

The woman's shoulders seemed to slump, and tears began forming in her eyes.

Ever-so-slowly, the woman retrieved Tigger and handed him to Diana. Never did we imagine that we'd actually be grateful for his repulsive trait of soaking our shirtfronts. But as he settled in to do his weaning thing, it served to validate that this was indeed our one-of-a-kind cat named Tigger.

I glanced at the sad-faced kids in the car, then over at Diana. We both knew what each other was thinking. We could make the two youngsters happy by turning Tigger over to them for keeps. Yet we were torn not merely because parting with our pet would cause us pain, but because a wandering stray had come to find love and comfort within our four walls. Was it selfish to keep Tigger for our own, or was it the best thing for this already-insecure bundle of nerves to head back to the place he considered home?

"Wait a minute," Diana said. Striding quickly over to our car, she reached through the open window and pulled something out. Returning, she said, "Do you mind if I give this stuffed bear to your children? I know it's not a real pet, but we want them to have *something*." In the foresight I'd come to appreciate in my wife, she'd brought this furry plaything along in anticipation of this moment.

The woman smiled. "Thanks, I'm sure they'll want to hold it on the way back home."

We chatted briefly, and by the time we parted ways, the tension of the ordeal had dissolved. As Diana and I went back toward our car, we noticed the woman's children smiling at us as they drove away. I guess it wasn't a perfect ending to the story, but it seemed reasonable, given our existence in an imperfect world. As for us, we were grateful to have Tigger back home, safe and sound.

In some ways, it flirts with the absurd to compare devotion to a pet with human relationships. Far too many parents experience relentless pain over not knowing the whereabouts of their children. For others, although physically present, a parent's despair sets in over the place where a child has chosen to take up residence spiritually. Still other parents could only wish that their child were still alive, so that love could be displayed without abandon.

Whatever your circumstances, our Savior longs to bring each of us home to Himself, to enfold us within His strong arms during our brightest days and darkest nights. Scripture paints this hope-filled picture: "Suppose each of you has a hundred sheep and loses one of them. Does he not leave the ninety-nine in the open country and go after the lost sheep until he finds it? And when he finds it, he joyfully puts it on his shoulders and goes home. Then he calls his friends and neighbors together and says, 'Rejoice with me; I have found my lost sheep'" (Luke 15:4-6).

As I've mentioned often in these pages, no family legacy is greater than that which instills within your loved ones' hearts an irresistible portrayal of Jesus and His love. But it can only happen as you choose to allow that same love to fill the recesses of your own soul. Because, in the end, you want to impart much more than "family values." You want to share your Spirit-empowered conviction that Jesus Christ, the searcher and Savior of lost souls, is the only way to know truth, and life abundant.

He awaits your call to begin the transformation of your heart into a grand repository of His grace. As that happens, Jesus Christ, working through you, will show those closest and dearest to you His unreserved love toward them, and His unwillingness to let them stay lost. And each time a wanderer comes home, it's party time.

"We had to celebrate and be glad . . . he was lost, and is found" (Luke 15:32).

Any way you look at it, there's no place like home.